80

TATTERED BATTLEMENTS

TATTERED BATTLEMENTS

A Fighter Pilot's Malta Diary
D-Day and After

Wing Commander
TIM JOHNSTON, DFC and Bar

*With an introduction
and notes by
CHAZ BOWYER*

WILLIAM KIMBER · LONDON

This revised edition first published in 1985 by
WILLIAM KIMBER & CO. LIMITED
100 Jermyn Street, London, SW1Y 6EE

© Mrs B. Johnston, 1943 and 1985

ISBN 0-7183-0547-7

The first part of this book was first published
anonymously in 1943 by Peter Davies under the
title *Tattered Battlements*: A Malta Diary by
A Fighter Pilot.

Photoset in North Wales by
Derek Doyle & Associates, Mold, Clwyd
and printed and bound in Great Britain by
Redwood Burn Limited, Trowbridge

TO HECTOR AND COBY
both killed in action

Contents

	Page
Foreword by Basil Collier	11
PART ONE:	
Introduction	13
Author's Foreword	17
Tattered Battlements: A Malta Diary	21
Notes to Part One	143
PART TWO:	
Introduction	149
D-Day and After	151
Notes to Part Two	213
Tim Johnson:	
Extract from *The Brazen Nose*	215
Index	219

List of Illustrations

		Page
The author in 1941	(*Mrs B. Johnston*)	16
The author at Brasenose College Oxford	(*Dr J.S. Owen*)	23
Squadron Leader Gracie	(*Westmacott*)	29
Spitfire flying off the deck	(*IWM*)	29
Messerschmitt Bf 109s over Takali	(*Daddo-Langlois*)	41
Spitfire on the runway, Malta	(*IWM*)	41
Harry Kelly, Wing Commander Stanley Grant, Spradley and Raoul Daddo-Langlois	(*Daddo-Langlois*)	43
Buck McNair	(*Daddo-Langlois*)	51
Pete Nash	(*Daddo-Langlois*)	51
Laddie Lucas	(*Daddo-Langlois*)	53
Norman MacQueen and Johnny Plagis	(*Daddo-Langlois*)	53
Patrick Schade	(*Daddo-Langlois*)	63
Soldiers and sailors refuelling a Spitfire	(*IWM*)	63
A Spitfire in its pen on Malta	(*C.G. Jefford*)	78
Buck Buchanan	(*Daddo-Langlois*)	87
Spitfires and Beaufighters on Malta	(*IWM*)	87
Building stone blast pens on Malta	(*IWM*)	98
Bomb-damaged Spitfire V	(*C.G. Jefford*)	98
Spitfires of 229 Squadron, October 1942	(*M.M. Stephens*)	109
Servicing a Spitfire in its pen	(*IWM*)	109
'Daddo-L' – Raoul Daddo-Langlois	(*Daddo-Langlois*)	125
'Bren' – Paul Brennan		125
The author in 1944	(*Mrs B. Johnston*)	153
Spitfires from 132 Wing providing fighter cover to the ground forces in France	(*IWM*)	163
Pilots of the Royal Norwegian Air Force in 132 Wing on a landing strip in France	(*IWM*)	163
The author gets some assistance	(*Mrs B. Johnston*)	165
The author when living under canvas	(*Mrs B. Johnston*)	185
The author off-duty	(*Mrs B. Johnston*)	203

*The publishers would like to thank Mr Christopher Shores for his help in
providing photographs to illustrate the author's Malta Diary.*

Foreword

by Basil Collier

In 1942 the Axis Powers planned to capture Malta as the prelude to a major offensive in North Africa. An advance to the Nile delta and a simultaneous thrust in Southern Russia would, they hoped, bring them a favourable decision by denying to the enemy the oil of the Middle East and the Caucasus. However eventually a projected airborne expedition to Malta was abandoned because Rommel's unexpectedly swift capture of Tobruk made it seem unnecessary. In the meantime the island was subjected to devastating air attacks.

The author of this book, flying his aircraft from the carrier *Eagle*, was one of the first sixteen Spitfire pilots to reach beleaguered Malta. Six weeks later he had scored a number of successes in face of almost overwhelming odds before his aircraft was shot down in flames. He lived to play a distinguished part in African affairs.

I have read many accounts of air battles. I do not know of one that gives a more vivid impression of what air combat in World War II was like, or which bears more clearly the stamp of intellectual honesty, integrity and candour.

1981

Basil Collier

11

Introduction

by Chaz Bowyer

Tattered Battlements was originally published as a slender volume in 1943, derived from a diary written by an RAF officer while serving on Malta during the spring of 1942. Due to wartime censorship, and indeed the custom of the period, the author was merely recorded as 'A Fighter Pilot'. He was, in fact, Hugh Anthony Stephen Johnston who ultimately became Wing Commander, CMG, OBE, DFC and Bar.

Born in Belfast on 7th December 1913, Tim Johnston (as he was always known), son of a member of the Indian Civil Service, was educated at King's School, Canterbury and Brasenose College, Oxford before joining the Colonial Service in 1936. On the outbreak of war in 1939 he returned to England and volunteered to join the RAF Volunteer Reserve, being enlisted in May 1940 and commissioned as a pilot on 27th September 1940. After further training at No 50 OTU, he joined his first operational unit, No 257 Squadron, at Coltishall, Norfolk to fly Hawker Hurricanes under the command of Squadron Leader R.R.S. (Bob) Tuck, DSO, DFC.

On 29th July 1941 a new squadron was officially formed at Coltishall, No 133 Squadron, the third 'Eagle' squadron to serve with the RAF and comprised almost wholly of 'neutral' American pilots, and Johnston, with promotion to Flight Lieutenant, was selected to become commander of 133 Squadron's 'A' Flight. A contemporary American of Johnston's flight described him thus: 'He worked us each and every day, somewhat along the lines of training we had undergone already, but with a great deal more purpose toward developing teamwork and individual efficiency'.*

---

* *The Eagle Squadrons* by V. Haugland; David & Charles, 1980

13

Johnston was to remain with the American squadron for the following seven months, during which time 133 was mainly based in Northern Ireland at Eglington, flying routine convoy escort patrols, but on 5th February 1942, while based at Kirton-in-Lindsey, Lincolnshire, Johnston shared in the destruction of a Dornier bomber. In the same month several American Eagle pilots began volunteering for active service in the Middle East campaign, including Tim Johnston, and in early March, as related in the following chapter, Johnston joined fifteen other pilots aboard a merchant ship bound for Gibraltar, where they were transferred, along with their crated Spitfires, aboard the aircraft carrier HMS *Eagle*. Finally, on 21st March 1942, led by Squadron Leader E.J. Gracie, DFC, all pilots flew off *Eagle*'s deck and set course for the besieged island of Malta.

Johnston's arrival on Malta came during a crucial phase of the aerial struggle for possession of the island. Malta, slightly less than 120 square miles of (mainly) rock island inhabited at that time by more than a quarter of a million citizens, lay a mere 60 miles from Axis-occupied Sicily, and the nearest Allied harbours were Alexandria, Egypt, some 820 miles to the east, and Gibraltar, virtually 1,000 miles westwards. Until 1940 Malta's prime value to Britain had been as a refuelling depot and dockyard for all shipping using the Suez Canal short cut routes to and from Far Eastern waters. Once Italy had declared war against the Allies in June 1940, the island immediately became a potentially key strategic vantage base for preventing Italian (and later, German) resupply convoys by air and/or sea to the North African coastal campaign areas. With both Allied and Axis military hierarchies fully aware of Malta's potential in this context, the island became the focal point of a prolonged and desperate naval and, particularly, aerial siege lasting almost exactly three years, during which time the Maltese population and its Allied defenders endured thousands of casualties, utter devastation of buildings and homes, near-starvation, and a continuing lack of virtually every amenity of a normal 'civilised' existence, during a total of more than 3,000 air attacks.

Throughout that ordeal were witnessed countless examples of supreme courage and tragic sacrifice, evidenced in the highest degree by the relative handful of young RAF pilots who provided Malta's primary defensive shield against the air onslaught. Operating in conditions which can only be termed primitive, those 'Few' unhesitatingly tackled vastly outnumbering odds in the sky over Malta daily, never flinching from attempting the seemingly impossible task of denying victory to the Axis airmen – and ultimately succeeding. Many of those young men arrived on the island untested in the crucible of kill-or-be-killed aerial combat, but within mere days – *if* they survived that long – they became hardened veterans, thoroughly inculcated with the fighting (and survival) tactics vital in the unique Malta air war. Though nominally a member of a particular unit – Tim Johnston was officially on the strength of No 126 Squadron – pilots were virtually part of a large pool, while individual aircraft were flown by whichever pilot was available when the order to 'scramble' was given; on Malta *everyone* was a defender.

When Johnston arrived on the island in late March 1942 Malta was about to be subjected to a prolonged, renewed Luftwaffe blitz campaign which did not wane (relatively speaking) until June, and in those months the RAF fighter pilots received their severest testing of the whole Malta air conflict. Action was continuous, the pace of fighting heightened, and individual survival seemed less as each dawn heralded yet another day of unceasing fighting. Within those few weeks many pilots were destined to die, while those who survived had experienced more action than they were to see during years of other forms of air operations. Some pilots became aces within days of commencing operations and received gallantry awards later in official recognition of their prowess, while others died without achieving public recognition, yet *every* pilot made a vital contribution to the eventual victory.

The author in 1941.

Author's Foreword

This diary was kept, sometimes under difficulties, in three exercise-books. When the contents were prepared for publication a certain amount of editing was found to be necessary: some entries, it was realised at once, had no hope of being passed by the censor; others might have passed the censor, unfamiliar with the peculiar conditions of the island, but have proved dangerous to those who are still fighting there; others, again, had lost what general interest they might once have possessed. These were all omitted. Finally, slight cuts have been made by the censor.

To balance these omissions, it was found that certain passages required amplification and connection to the rest of the story if they were to prove readily intelligible. This should perhaps have been done by the use of footnotes or explanatory passages.

It was thought, however, that a multitude of these would spoil the flow of the story and would be a source of irritation to the reader. Those passages, therefore, in which the sense was obscured by over-abbreviation, or by the use of terms or references not generally known, were re-written in such a way that they could be understood by all. The style of the context was retained. In other cases, where the description of some event or personality seemed to call for elaboration for the benefit of those who did not know the island or its pilots, a similar liberty was taken.

The danger of making these changes was realised and particular care was taken that no exaggeration or departure from the truth should be admitted with them. The current alarms and rumours, together with certain good but unlikely stories, have been related, because they formed part of our lives, but an effort has been made to indicate the credibility of each. The temptation to overpaint the picture, exaggerate success, minimise or excuse failure, has been sternly resisted: the story of the island's siege is vivid enough as it is, and this particular record of it, having little to commend it but its honesty, must stand or fall by that quality. If there are any inaccuracies they will have crept in through misinformation or because the diary was not always made up, as it should have been, at the end of each day.

The passages not in diary form, except those dealing with the hospital, were added after the rest had been accepted for publication. The descriptions of the last combat, and of the preceding days, as well as those of life in hospital, were written during convalescence in Malta and England, when most of the revisionary work was also completed.

The names of those who were killed have not, by intention, been changed or omitted. It is profoundly hoped that this decision will cause no unnecessary suffering; perhaps, on the contrary, since the manner of their passing became them and their Service so well, a record of it may bring, not sorrow, but strength and comfort to those to whom they belonged.

March 1943

PART ONE

Tattered Battlements

A Malta Diary

I

The *Queen Victoria* had nothing in common with her distinguished royal contemporaries; she was a merchant-man and looked like thousands of other freighters – fo'c'sle, hold, bridge, hold, funnel, hold, stern. We had slipped down the river in her on a perfect afternoon in February, when a pale sun had been shining through the smoke and haze that hung over the river to light soft sparkles on its surface.

We had known that we were going overseas, but the CO alone knew where it was to be. The rest of us could only speculate, basing our guesses on some rather baffling instructions which we had received for the disposal of our baggage. The best bet seemed to be Malta, but there were certain factors which pointed elsewhere, and the Near or Far East were both possibilities.

We had been whisked away from our British squadrons on overseas posting at no more than 48 hours' notice. All we knew was that the amount of luggage which we were allowed shrank at every stage of the journey until it reached a nadir of 10 lbs, and that somewhere in the holds of the ship, packed in crates, there was a Spitfire apiece for us.

We had tried to pump the CO, but to no purpose; all he would say was that we should soon know and that there would be no lack of action. Some of us were sorry to be leaving home, others glad. Bart, my fellow Flight Commander, had been married less than a week, and would naturally have preferred to stay at home; on the other hand Mac and Jimmie were missing their American sun and were glad to go anywhere so long as it was south, while Australia was sanguine enough to believe that he might be on his way home. I didn't know what to think. I had reasons for wanting to stay at home, but I felt that we were embarked for something I would not willingly have missed.

As soon as we were free of land, the CO had assembled us all and told us our destination and what was expected of us. It was Malta, and we were to fly to it the second batch of Spitfires ever to be sent overseas; there was certain to be hard fighting ahead of us, and we must all prepare ourselves in every way so as to be ready to engage in it when it came.

The ship was no greyhound and the voyage gave us a chance to take stock of each other and shake down together. We were sixteen pilots. The CO, Bart and I, and five others were British; Mac and Jimmie were Americans; there was one New Zealander, one Australian and four Canadians.

We found that our experience varied enormously. The CO and Bart alone among us had fought in the Battle of Britain; of the rest only three had destroyed enemy aircraft, and there were some who had not only not been in action, but had not even seen their first Hun.

I think we were all somewhat exasperated at our slow rate of progress. If we could have flown, we should have been at Gib in six hours; as it was we should be lucky to be there inside a fortnight. This impatience was heightened one morning, just as we were running into warmer latitudes, when we heard that air battles had been fought all the previous day over Malta and that seventeen enemy aircraft had been destroyed or damaged. I think we were all terrified that the fighting might be over before we arrived, and we passed much time reckoning the earliest day we could expect to get there. I remember I realised that the 1914-15 volunteers had had the same fear, and I wondered whether our case would prove to be the same as theirs. It seemed unlikely, and anyway I was too excited at the prospect of intensive fighting to spend much time over theoretical speculation.

We messed with the ship's officers; they were all Scots and, although our invasion of their quarters made conditions far from comfortable for them, they were friendliness itself. We could never get them to say more than a few words at a time; they seemed to be faintly self-conscious, but they were so transparently straightforward and simple, that I think we all felt they were better men than we were.

I found it curious that the two elements, sea and air, should

Photographed when he was at Brasenose College, Oxford, the author is third from the left in the front row.

attract such opposite types. They were as different from us as they well could be. We were talkative, they taciturn; we were volatile, they steady-going and self-effacing; we were quick-witted, they slow-thinking; we were opportunists, they routine workers.

I wondered whether the seafaring type had always been as they were, or whether, after it had become an established calling, the sea had attracted this steadier type of man. Perhaps when the sea was a little-explored element, the sailors had been like us, and not like them. If Flecker was right, and Odysseus was a talkative, bald-headed seaman who 'with great lies about his wooden horse set the crew laughing and forgot his course' then the type had changed. In that description Odysseus is pure fighter-pilot. Possibly these differences between us were superficial rather than fundamental, because we stood at opposite ends of our two trades, and in essentials we perhaps shared the same ground; if not, I did not see how we agreed so well together, and how we could feel so much respect for them. Probably we were their prototypes.

Some days later we ran up the narrowing bottle-neck between Europe and Africa and at dusk arrived safely in Gibraltar roads. At first it appeared that we should have to spend the night outside, but when our identity was established the harbour was opened to us, and we were almost ushered inside. One felt that the footman had missed the title when we first presented our card, and was now effusively repairing his mistake.

For a week at Gib we lived in the *Eagle*, with nothing to do but amuse ourselves, while the ground-crews, under the direction of Shorty Hughes, worked day and night, but mostly by night, in the sultry heat of the ship's hangar, to assemble and test our aircraft. We swam, ate and drank, and pottered about the town, while every day the papers told of increasingly heavy attacks on Malta. We all sensed it was the lull before the storm, and I think most of us, while making the most of the moment, were busy bracing ourselves in spirit for the ordeal which we knew to be just ahead.

This bracing process, though at the time it was subterranean, assumes in retrospect its position as the most important of all our activities during this period. Beside it the silk stockings we bought in the town, the John Collins we drank in the numerous bars, and our baths in the chilled waters of Sandy Bay, have paled in memory. We knew that we should not be too late.

One day we heard we were to move, and that night the *Eagle* got under way and, with her escort, slipped out of harbour.

Saturday 21.3.42

Called at 0515; I'd woken up early as I usually do before an important day. Went up to the flight-deck to supervise the stowage of the rest of my belongings in my aircraft; we were allowed ten pounds for the flight, which covered bare essentials but no more. Was glad to find just the right amount of wind; if there had been too much it would have been too rough for us to take off, and if too little mightn't have been possible at all: the *Eagle*'s flight-deck is only 450 feet long, which isn't much for Spits. On the surface the wind seemed to be blowing from the east, but higher up it was said to be westerly and therefore favourable. Hope those Met people know what they are talking about, it's a hell of a long way to fly in a head wind.

It was just after dawn, and the weather looked uncertain; the sky was two to three parts overcast with banks of cloud at what appeared to be many different levels. I hoped to goodness we should get off, if we didn't it might mean a week's delay. There was a strong wind blowing over the flight-deck, and the Spits, huddled together in the stern, looked as if they might be swept overboard at any moment.

Climbing up to the deck was quite an ordeal and once there you felt you must be very careful not to miss your footing or you would be whisked away for sure. It was a high, remote place and did not seem to be part of the ship; if we were torpedoed it was difficult to believe that it too would sink.

Down to breakfast and heard that a start was expected at 0705; didn't dare drink anything and thought bream made a pretty poor send-off. All went on deck and received the final instructions: 'A' Flight was to go off in the first batch – you needn't worry about that, chaps, it's a piece of cake, the last lot had no difficulty at all – and form up as quickly as we could; when we were all set to go, the ship would flash a white light and the leader, in this case the CO, would set course; all we had to do was to follow him. We ought to begin to be careful near Bizerta, the French sometimes sent fighters out and you never knew what they might do; while passing Pantellaria it was advisable to keep a bloody good look-out. They had RDF there and a squadron of 109s. When we got to Malta we weren't to land at Takali, as originally planned, but at Luqa; that was the big aerodrome just south of Valetta, we could miss it. And for God's sake, chaps, don't try to take off in coarse pitch.

We all climbed into our machines, strapped ourselves in and began to wait. The sea was getting up; occasionally a shower of spray would sweep over the deck and drench the aircraft, but in the cockpits we were snug and dry. The ground crews stood round to see us off. They had been working intensively for ten days in most difficult conditions, but now their ordeal was over and ours was just beginning; you could see they felt like a football crowd and you couldn't grudge it to them. It was a remarkable feat: the aircraft had come to them in pieces, packed in crates, and in a week they had assembled them, working in the cramped conditions of the *Eagle*'s hangar, with only inches to spare between one machine and its neighbour, and they had adjusted and tested not only the engines, but the R/T, cannons, hydraulics, the electrical and compressed-air systems, oxygen, instruments and everything else. I asked my fitter whether everything was going to work and he was cheerfully reassuring.

The ships were zigzagging continuously; one minute the *Malaya* would be on the starboard bow, the next she would appear to port; the *Hermione* was out ahead and destroyers guarded our flanks. Seven o'clock came and went.

Wished we'd been able to get away without this delay; I'd felt quite happy about it earlier, but now I found myself beginning to think of all the difficulties, the take-off, the distance over the sea, the 1095 at Pantellaria. Suppose the undercart failed to retract properly; it meant trying to land back on the carrier. I looked at the deck and tried to decide whether I could put a Spit down on it. Barnes had had a faulty oil-pump and had landed safely, but that was in a Hurricane. It would be rather a triumph to bring a Spit down safely but very difficult. I couldn't make up my mind, and told myself not to be a b. f., I wouldn't have to, anyway. That was the worst of waiting, your courage always ebbed away. I was beginning to hope we shouldn't go after all, when there was a burst of activity up forward.

The CO, who was to be first off, started his engine, but a minute later it stopped again; after a slight delay he re-started it and taxied out; the flag dropped, he opened his throttle, flew down the deck and disappeared under the bow. I couldn't see anything from where I was, so watched the expressions of the airmen, and after what seemed a long interval saw them break into smiles, next instant a very small aeroplane staggered into view about half a mile in front of the ship. Heard afterwards that the CO very nearly hit the drink; not surprising, he'd only flown a Spit once before. Boulton, second off, went to the other extreme and almost did a stall turn as he crossed the bows. All the rest were normal.

My turn was next to last. I taxied out and waited for all the temperatures to reach the right marks, made sure the airscrew was in fine pitch, held the brakes for a moment as I opened up, and then let her go. I pushed the stick hard forward and the tail came up at once. I could see where I was going now and had no difficulty in keeping the machine straight, aimed at the marker-flag in the forward ack-ack position, or just to the right of it, and felt myself airborne a few yards before I ran out of deck. There was a violent eddy, like hitting a slipstream, as the aircraft crossed the bows, but then it settled down into normal though sluggish flight. Raised the undercart and watched nervously to see whether it would function properly, heard it click home and was relieved to see the red light showing that it had locked; that was one problem less. At 1,000 feet the change-over to the auxiliary tank had to be faced; did it very carefully, thinking how silly I'd look if I jettisoned it by mistake – the two levers were adjacent – and waited to see whether it was going to function. I knew nothing about the mechanism so I sat and called on my reserves of faith in things I didn't understand, and after half a minute reckoned the danger period was over and I could relax; that was another problem less.

Glanced down at the fleet; even from 1,500 feet the ships seemed very widely spaced and astonishingly small; no wonder bombs miss. As for landing on the *Eagle*, it was out of the question – like trying to land on a matchbox. The ships which before had seemed safe and friendly had suddenly become remote and inaccessible, and I felt it was useless to look to them for help now, we were in a different element and there was no more they could do for us.

All this time I had been watching the others very closely, not wishing to find myself suddenly alone, and by cutting corners had managed to catch them in one circuit; the CO immediately straightened out and set course towards the east. I looked round and counted only five Spits, including myself; there should have been nine of us; counted again to make sure, still only five, so called the CO on the R/T and told him; heard him say 'Okay, Okay' quite cheerfully, wasn't sure whether he knew or not, but involved conversation over the R/T is impossible, so I shut up. The ship had given us the white light, the people on board should know, and I supposed the other four were all right. Spent the first ten minutes watching the important gauges on the instrument panel, they could have been more steady. Noticed we had climbed to 8,000 feet and flattened out there; the weather still appeared uncertain, with large banks of hazy clouds at different levels, but on the whole the tendency seemed to be to improve.

I looked down on the tiny corrugations below to try to see whether the waves were breaking from east or west, but the distance was too great; reflected that we should know soon enough if the wind was foul. After an hour's flying the African coast showed up clearly to starboard; it looked mountainous and blue. We flew past the Galite Island, about twenty miles off the mainland; a solitary lighthouse was the only sign of habitation and a heavy sea breaking against steep-to cliffs made them look pretty unfriendly. However, we were some minutes ahead of schedule and that was encouraging. At Bizerta the mountains began to recede inland; at the same time the weather improved and we flew out into sunshine and endless visibility. Ahead of us, beyond Cape Bon, we could see Pantellaria: I'd always thought of it as a small rock, but it proved to be not unlike the Isle of Man, with a mountain at the southern end and a low-lying plain to the north. This was the dangerous stage, so I opened the hood for better vision, and prodded myself into vigilance. The sun was fairly high by now, and both sea and sky a beautiful, vivid blue; on our right a convoy was creeping down the Tunisian coast towards Susa, which showed up as a white blur ahead. Gave a routine glance at the instrument-panel and noticed a red light, that meant the auxiliary tank was running dry; at the same moment the engine began to lose power, so I quickly flipped back

Squadron Leader Gracie (centre), when a flight Lieutenant with 56 Squadron in February 1941. On the left is Sergeant Hillwood and the right PO Higginson.

Spitfire flying off the deck.

on to the main tanks and it caught at once. Noted how long we'd been flying; Malta was not more than an hour ahead, so the fuel situation was splendid.

Left Pantellaria behind and began the last long stretch across the sea to Malta. Presently we could see cumulus clouds ahead, we'd been told these usually formed over the island during the day; soon Gozo's perpendicular cliffs came into view, behind them Malta's. The two islands appeared flat and of the same thickness, like sections cut from a tree trunk, but their colouring – a rich honey – looked beautiful against the background of blue. The CO called the Malta homing-station to announce our approach and could hear them warning us to be careful because there were 110s over the island. When we were still ten miles out we could see pillars of dust and smoke from bomb-bursts; clearly we'd arrived in the middle of a raid; that was appropriate and rather exciting. As we flew in low I was struck by the apparent density of the population and by the beauty of the local stone.

We all landed safely at Luqa and later were joined by our four renegades. We had flown a long way. I had a slight head-ache, felt stiff, and glad it was over. We took our kit out of the machines and waited for instructions; the aerodrome was hot and dusty and no one seemed to know what to do with us. At last an officer appeared and took us off to lunch in the mess and afterwards we learnt that Takali would be our parent aerodrome, and that we should live in a mess which was pointed out to us. After lunch and a further wait, a bus arrived to take us there.

We had made about half the distance, when we realised there was another air-raid in progress; the bus pulled up opposite a heavy ack-ack site and we all got out to watch. A group of deeply sun-burned Tommies joined us; we hardly knew what to expect, but tried to appear as nonchalant as they. Soon the barrage opened, there was a crack like a whip as the guns near us fired and a prolonged swish as the shells went boring up. The raiders were coming in from the north at about 15,000 feet; it was almost as if they were popping out of a hole in the sky into view; you would see one, and then another, who hadn't been visible at all when you'd first noticed the leader, would appear from nowhere behind him, and so on with a third and a fourth.

As they came nearer us we could see them to be Ju 88s; the occasional specks behind, weaving this way and that, were too small to identify but must have been the escort of Me 109s. The guns seemed accurate, but the bandits came on undismayed and passed almost overhead; we saw there were eighteen in the wave. They broke formation to dive on their target, Takali aerodrome, and come down in a regularly-spaced string, like children sliding down a banister. Noticed that the guns didn't seem to go near them in the dive, or as they pulled out, but became more accurate again as they headed back towards Sicily.

After the first waves there was a brief lull before another eighteen followed and repeated the same attack. Someone said the guns had got one; apparently the pilot or controls must have been hit, because it never pulled out of its dive, but went on into the ground; three of the crew baled out, and we heard later that one of them had landed in the middle of the aerodrome. There were no friendly fighters anywhere, which was rather humiliating.

We were beginning to think it was all over, when the guns opened up again, this time towards the south-east, and another bunch of eighteen came in and unloaded over Takali. The plot must have been 50 plus; this was obviously going to be the real McCoy.

We continued the journey, passed through a heavy stone gateway and pulled up before an imposing mansion. A Wing-Co met us, introduced himself as the Station Commander, apologised that he couldn't wait and turning to his companion said, 'Well, Doc, are you feeling brave?' Both of them rode away on a motor-bike. We soon discovered the reason for this; they were going to recover and try to identify the bodies of the officers who had just been killed in the raid we'd been watching; heard that one of the victims was Baker, formerly of 257.

Learnt that the mansion was to be our mess. It was a fine house built in the local style, round a central courtyard. There was a wide stone staircase, with a massive balustrade, the rooms were high and delightfully cool, and on the flat roof we found a charming little garden and a terrace commanding a magnificent view.

Met old friends in Norman and Denis and adjourned to the bar to hear all their news. Denis has been in the island for a long time; he said after the *Illustrious* had left last year there had been little activity until December, when the Hun had reappeared in Sicily. At first he'd operated on a small scale, and in conjunction with the Italians, but gradually the Italians had fallen out of the picture and the German effort had increased. Raids had been frequent, and were always heavily escorted, but there had been nothing massive until yesterday at dusk, when fifty 88s had bombed Takali. That's why we'd been diverted to land at Luqa this morning. What we'd just seen was the repeat performance. What was the fighting like? Bloody hot; it looked simple enough, to see the 88s come in as they had this afternoon, but there was always a cloud of 109s sitting up above them, and another waiting for them off-shore; what we'd have to get used to was being heavily outnumbered.

I thought Denis looked older than when I'd last seen him and later someone told me what had happened to him. While attacking E-boats he'd been shot down by a Macchi, had baled out and come down in the sea not far from one of the boats he'd helped to cripple; no help had arrived, so he'd abandoned his dinghy, swum over to it and climbed on board; all the crew were dead and everything was drenched in blood, but as he'd discarded his dinghy he was obliged to stay there until picked up some hours later.

Told that of the six 110s which we'd been warned against this morning, four had been shot down by the Hurricanes. Our 'B' Flight haven't shown up yet, but there's a chance they may come to-morrow.

All arrangements for our reception disorganised by a stray bomb, but it appears we shall sleep in what used to be the Accounts Section and share this mess with 249. All felt sleepy, so grabbed salvage blankets and made beds on the floor.

II

Sunday 22.3.42

All rather aggrieved to find that the aircraft, which each had regarded as his own, to cherish or modify as he pleased, belonged to the island and not to the individual or squadron, but as conditions became clearer it was realised that this was a necessity. 249, after combat and bombing on the ground, had only one aircraft serviceable; we had nine and there were said to be half a dozen Hurricanes, not a formidable total. Pilots were more plentiful, the proportion worked out to about three to each machine; as no spares or replacements of aircraft were available, this figure looked as if it would increase. Still no sign of 'B' Flight, so we had to presume that they'd failed to get away and were on their way back to Gibraltar; the Navy wouldn't want to hang about for long.

We had found, in daylight, that the mansion made a good mess; lack of a proper ante-room compensated by a spacious flat-roof, which made a delightful place in which to sit in the sun. Looking out from it you could see, laid out below, the whole eastern part of the island: straight ahead were Grand Harbour and the Sliema Creek, with Valetta between them, and the towns of Vittoriosa, Senglea, Cospicua, Floriana and Sliema grouped round in a semi-circle; to one side of these Luqa aerodrome, where we'd landed yesterday, could be picked out clearly by its runways; beyond it lay Halfar aerodrome and the naval base of Calafrana; in the foreground was Takali aerodrome. In sunshine this view, in its colouring, detail, and lucidity, reminded me of a painting by Canaletto. I was struck again by the beauty of the local stone; its shades vary from a rich honey to cold grey and it is said to harden as it weathers. When newly cut it is so soft that the masons shape it with axes and finish it with planes;

new or seasoned it has a beautiful texture and colouring, and it gives the houses here a distinction that their architecture doesn't always deserve.

I spent the day questioning those who had flown in the island and knew something of local form and Hun tactics; heard many points of view, but all agreed that conditions were unique. I gathered that before a raid patrols of 109s circled the island, that the bombers normally came in with close escort at about 15,000 feet, dived to 5,000 to drop their bombs, and that their withdrawal was always covered by further patrols operating off the coast. This sounded more tricky than any of us had imagined. Everyone we spoke to stressed that we should always be heavily outnumbered and that it was extraordinarily difficult to attack the bombers; if the early patrols failed to pick you up, they said, the close escort would do so and would engage you long enough for the bombers to reach the protective cordon of 109s waiting off-shore. To disregard this cordon and to make a practice of chasing the bombers far towards Sicily would very soon prove fatal; you had to try to knock them down over the island. If you were shot down into the sea you might or might not be picked up; there was an air-sea rescue service, but the boat had been so badly shot-up by 109s some time before that it couldn't always be expected to go out. The ack-ack was good and wouldn't often mistake you for a Hun, but you had to look out for the 109s from the moment you took off until after you'd touched down again; a Hurricane had almost been shot down the other day as he came in to land.

Until then the policy had been for the Spits to provide high cover for the Hurricanes, whose role it was to attack the bombers. This system hadn't been altogether successful: not many of the Hurricanes were armed with cannon, and machine-guns were proving ineffective against the heavily armoured 88s; moreover, the Spits, always outnumbered, would sometimes be compelled to engage one lot of 190s, and so leave the Hurricanes open to attack by another. Since their arrival three weeks before, few bombers had been shot down, while 249, whose engagements had been almost exclusively with 109s, had only destroyed five enemy aircraft, plus probables, for the loss of four of their own.

I felt convinced that these tactics were wrong and found almost everyone was of the same opinion. They were in fact on the point of being abandoned. If we'd had enough fighters to decimate his fighter strength in Sicily they might have succeeded, because he couldn't then have sent his bombers over inadequately escorted without courting disastrous losses; but as things were, our fighter strength was meagre at the start and there was no prospect of rapid reinforcement, therefore any war of attrition was bound to go against us. Moreover, it was the bombers which were doing the damage, it was they which should be destroyed; the loss of a few 109s would not deter the Hun, but a drain of 88s, more valuable in themselves and in their crews, might stop him.

We discussed it carefully and agreed that both Spits and Hurricanes should do everything possible to avoid combat with the 109s, or, if engaged by them, at least conserve their ammunition as much as they possibly could for the more important target of the bombers. When we were only able to put up perhaps four Spits and four Hurricanes against raids of 80 plus, it seemed doubly necessary to concentrate the whole of so small a force on one objective. It would mean increased risks for us; as our aircraft went in to attack, each would have to pick its own target and operate individually, so that the force as a whole could deploy its maximum effort, and during this time they would be wide open to attack by all three groups of 109s, but the increased results should more than off-set the higher losses. The utmost vigilance would be necessary; anyone who relaxed for even a few seconds, or became too absorbed in his quarry, would be endangering himself. The loss of a pilot would be less serious than the loss of an aircraft; it wasn't so at home, but it was so here and everyone must recognise the fact. There were to be no heroics but scientific and calculated fighting. What was needed was not a glorious episode in the island story, but good arithmetic, that is, high gains and low losses.

There were a few who shook their heads over these tactics and prophesied failure, but we had talked it all out after gleaning what information we could from those who had been here longer than we had and everyone agreed with the CO's conclusions. They were adopted by 126 from the very beginning and proved successful.

Clearly the outcome of the operation would depend very largely on our ability to avoid the offensive patrol of 109s sent out in advance to clear the way for the bombers. The obvious plan seemed to be to climb, not over the island, but south of it. When we put this forward we were told that it had already been tried without success, because the Hun patrolled that area more heavily than any other. We were inclined to believe that the old hands were shooting a line, and remained cheerfully unconvinced.

We heard that there was a convoy coming in and that we should begin work next day. Takali was still unserviceable after the bombing, so we should be operating from Luqa. Norman took me to Valetta in the afternoon; I cabled my safe arrival home and had a look round the town, which appeared prosperous and little damaged. We went to the Monico for tea, but no sooner had the food been brought than the sirens sounded and it was promptly snatched away again and we were hustled outside. Norman was furious; apparently exactly the same thing happened to him last time he came here. We returned to M'dina in the evening in a gharry. Near Takali the ground was thick with bomb-craters and red flags denoting DAs. At one of these the animal shied; the driver stuck his head round the corner of the cab and observed, not without pride, 'horsey he smell bombey'.

Monday 23.3.42
Came to dawn readiness at Luqa, strong wind from east with low cloud, mist and very poor visibility. Convoy from Middle East was coming in, with Spits and Hurricanes, operating in pairs, protecting it; muffled rumble of bombs and gunfire from direction of the sea showed that Luftwaffe was already at work. Mike and I – second pair off – got away at 0910 and flew out east in the direction in which we thought the ships were. Weather was so thick that we lost sight of the coast almost as soon as we'd crossed it and for a few minutes saw nothing, until a big merchantman suddenly loomed up ahead with a destroyer or light cruiser in front of her; that was all the convoy we could see.

We began to orbit at a respectful distance and had completed less than half a circuit when vivid flashes from the escort showed that she had opened up on something. I thought it was at us, so turned outwards hard and began to kick on rudder to try to fox the gunners, then noticed that the barrage was being put up ahead of the ships, not to starboard where we were, and there in the middle of it, right down on the water, and flying slowly, was a Ju 88. I headed for him at once and quickly closed in; saw him fire a recognition light, which burst in three red stars (suppose this was meant to deceive), but at same moment he turned and gave a silhouette in plan-view so there could be no doubt about his identity. I followed him in his turn and opened fire with a 1½-sec burst of cannon and machine-gun at 80 yards; deflection was for 60 degrees so he was actually under my nose and I couldn't see the results until I'd broken; pleased to find that his starboard engine was giving off a stream of white smoke. He continued to climb, and take evasive action, making for the great banks of cloud above. I fired three more 2-sec bursts with cannon and machine-guns at 200 yards from quarter astern, but without seeing any results; knew it wasn't good attack for an 88, but with cloud-cover so near it was a race against time, and to get him at all I had to get him quickly.

Starboard engine was still smoking, leaving a thin white stream of glycol vapour, but he appeared to be flying strongly. Suddenly he pulled up very steeply in a final effort, with me still hanging on to his flanks, and managed to reach the first patch of cloud; he disappeared, reappeared, disappeared again. He had been twisting and turning this way and that and I realised that I had lost all sense of direction and that we were probably far out over the sea. The cloud was more solid here and I thought I'd lost him for good; one part of me was cursing like hell for letting him slip away, while another was wondering whether my R/T was working, where I was, whether I should ever be able to find the island again in such poor visibility, and whether I'd been hit by his return fire.

Continued to hunt about for him in the broken cloud and had almost given up, when spotted him below and slightly ahead, running from one piece of cloud-cover to the next; came in dead astern this time, took careful aim and finished off my cannon ammunition in him; broke away and found that both his motors were now giving off white smoke. As I watched three objects suddenly fell away from the fuselage; thought at first that the aircraft was beginning to break up, and felt surprised that this should happen so long after my burst, then realised it was probably the crew jumping out. Three little black specks had been silhouetted for a moment against the cloud, before they disappeared into it; wondered what it was that had made them exchange their cabin for the almost certain death of a rough sea twenty miles from land.

The aircraft fell away in a right-hand spiral dive and disappeared into cloud; I followed, emerged underneath and at first saw only an expanse of dirty grey sea, with endless white horses; then looking round picked out a patch of burning petrol. Felt none of the exultation I'd experienced last year with my first kill, just satisfaction at having completed the job.

Called Woodie on the R/T and said: 'I've got him, I've got him.' Woodie came back 'Good show, good show.' I then transmitted for a homing, and at the same time checked all the vital gauges to make sure I hadn't been hit in the engine. Found them all correct and steady; that was a mercy, because there wasn't much hope of rescue from that sea. Followed Woodie's 180° and emerged over the island, landed at Luqa. Inspected the aircraft for hits and found two machine-gun strikes in the loading-edges of the wings; I hadn't noticed any return fire while I had been attacking, but was concentrating on the deflection rather than the target; had fired six-seconds' ammunition; not spectacular, but good enough.

Mike, naturally rather chagrined, had revenge when we went off again later in the day; this time he saw an 88 which I missed. He dived at it from quarter astern and got in a very good burst with strikes in the cockpit and both engines, then polished it off with two head-on attacks. That was two 88s destroyed, while 249 had secured a probable and Jimmie a damaged; no losses.

Later met Killeen, who had just arrived in the convoy. The ship in which he was had two extraordinary escapes. Don't envy the crews their jobs, sitting over a cargo of petrol and bombs. Heard that the Luftwaffe used 70 aircraft, nearly all bombers; if only we had more ourselves!

Tuesday 24.3.42

Mac and Jimmie each got their first in the morning; sent up together against two 109 bombers, Woodie gave them perfect interception and they jumped them. Mac's blew up almost at once, but Jimmie's gave him some trouble before it went in. Both delighted; right and proper that they should notch their first on the same day, because they joined up together in the States, trained together, went to England together, to 121 together, and came here together.

Complete contrast in every way: Mac fair, Jimmie dark; Mac tall, Jimmie short; Mac burly, Jimmie slight; Mac garrulous, Jimmie (for an American) reserved; Mac a New Englander, Jimmie a Californian. They are old friends, but argue incessantly; even do their bitching differently, Mac noisily and profanely, Jimmy quietly and lovingly. To-day Mac, who can never keep his mouth shut, had called up on the R/T and said: 'Hello, Peck, Mac here. I've knocked mine down; do I have to come and help you with yours?' Jimmie's answer gave joy to all in Fighter Control Room who heard it.

Went on readiness at 1 p.m.; found only couple of aircraft serviceable, so rang up Woodie and told him. He asked if two of us would be prepared to take off and try to disorganise a raid which would be coming in shortly. We enquired if there would be any Hurricanes, and were told no, none were serviceable, it would have to be just the two of us, but there was no need to go if we thought it was asking too much. We said Okay, we'd have a crack at it. Woodie advised us to climb south of the island and said he would try to bring us into the raiders head-on before they reached their target; he thought we might be able to scatter some of them. Took off with Mike and headed south, weather was perfect with a dazzling sun, and sea and sky as blue as each other. Climbed 6,000 feet, when four 109s passed overhead, flying west, in wide line abreast, but didn't see us; gained another 2,000 feet, when two fresh 109s arrived, spotted us, and circled overhead, always just out of reach.

Climbed on to 10,000 feet, flat out but very warily, when Mike suddenly spun and lost half his angels; suppose I must have been climbing too fast for him. Didn't know what to do now, whether to climb on up by myself and accept risk of our each being picked off individually, or to lose time by going down and joining Mike. Problem solved itself; found I had been so busy keeping my eye on the two 109s that I had lost sight of Mike, so I dived towards land, gave my two shadowers the slip, and began to climb again. Almost at once more 109s appeared and circled over me, four immediately above and two farther away; think they suspected a trap, because for some minutes they watched and waited. At last one of them decided to attack; he came down very fast and almost head-on; at about 400 yards he opened fire and at the same time dropped his starboard wing as if he were going to do a roll to the right. As he flashed by within 50 yards he was past vertical and was going so fast that as soon as he began to pull out of his dive vapour trails appeared behind his wing-tips. As he opened fire I had been able to watch the patterns of bluish smoke in front of him; they looked rather like paper streamers being thrown out and it was difficult to believe that there was anything lethal about them. The others followed his example, but came down individually so that I was able to turn in to each one and take the attack head-on or on the beam; some fired; some didn't; none stayed to fight, but there were enough of them to keep me as busy as a one-armed paper-hanger. I gave one of them, which was doing its usual stall-turn after the attack, a short burst, but more to relieve my feelings than in hope of hitting him; realised it was foolish – he was right out of range – and decided to keep the rest of my ammunition.

Continued to play with them a little longer, then realised original plan was no longer feasible. So much for my theory: had tried to gain height south of the island and had climbed into the thick of the 109s, as predicted. Did an aileron turn and found I'd managed to shake them off; felt very tired from throwing the aircraft about, and had no idea what was happening. Gondar had been giving instructions, but I'd been too occupied to pay attention.

Flew inland towards Grand Harbour, where original attack was expected, looking for some signs of raiders, and wondering what had happened to Mike, whether he was all right. Grand Harbour seemed peaceful, when I suddenly noticed bombs bursting all over Halfar and intense barrage of light flak. Aircraft were pulling out of their dives and flying away south in a compact bunch; couldn't see what they were at first, then noticed fixed undercarriages, which meant Stukas. Felt this was a terrific opportunity, if only I could get among them without being seen by the 109s, which were sure to be hanging about somewhere near. Remembered someone had told me that trouble with Stukas was that one always overshot them, so pulled the throttle well back and flew in dead astern of the formation. Took furtive looks all round for 109s, but couldn't see any; that was too good to last, so opened on the nearest Stuka from 100 yards with both cannon and machine-guns. Can remember promising myself something spectacular – small fragments or a sheet of flame – but all that came were some vivid flashes from

Messerschmitt Bf 109s over Takali.

Spitfire on the runway, Malta.

exploding cannon-shells and a stream of white smoke from his belly. I was so over-confident that I pulled out to one side, instead of breaking away properly, and sat there watching him; it was probably then that I got hit, if not by him then by one of his nearer friends. By this time we were out over the sea, and I knew the 109s wouldn't be far, so I quickly gave him another 3-second burst from the port quarter; think I allowed too much deflection, because he still kept flying, though he was beginning to lag behind the others and there was more glycol streaming out than before. I knew he couldn't get home, so broke off and flew back to the island; a last look showed him farther behind the formation than before and still trailing his white plume.

Returned to Luqa, entered circuit, dropped wheels and was about to lower flaps when I noticed light flak bursting above me, at the same time an incoherent transmission came over the R/T. I thought there must be a 109 gunning somewhere, and that it would be a wise precaution to put my wheels up, but couldn't see him anywhere, and didn't want to appear to panic, so tried to spot him first. Looked round again, and this time saw him at 500 yards on the port beam, flying towards me; whipped my wheels up and stuffed my nose down at the same time; as I did so he opened fire, but I felt fairly certain he wouldn't hit me. He flashed past, did a stall turn and came back towards me, but didn't attack again. I followed him north-west; knew I couldn't catch him, and that I hadn't much ammunition left, but thought I might be able to jump him later if he decided to go ground-strafing; possibly I was feeling bloody-minded at being attacked over my own base. I was about 1,000 feet below him and half a mile astern, heading for some cloud-cover from which to watch him, when he returned and started a diving head-on attack; seeing it coming, I pulled up hard, in something between a loop and a climbing turn, towards a cloud to port. I continued to watch him over the side of the cockpit and knew he'd opened fire when the sinister blue tendrils shot out of his wings towards me; saw him follow me round in my turn and the deflection looked about right. This time I didn't feel a bit confident of not being hit. The aircraft had lost so much speed that the evasive action I tried to take as I saw him firing was sluggish and ineffective; the cloud had failed me by coming no nearer, and I felt as if I'd been

Harry Kelly, Wing Commander Stanley Grant, Spradley and Raoul Daddo-Langlois.

dangled at the end of a piece of string for him to shoot at. He had flashed past behind me before I reached the cloud and then I stalled almost at once. Didn't realise until afterwards that I then fulfilled all the conditions described by the legendary fighter pilot: 'There I was, on my back, in cloud, with nothing on the clock, still climbing ...' Resisted temptation to hold the stick back, and fell out very slowly; looked carefully everywhere, but the 109 had disappeared, so returned to Luqa and landed, a good one in spite of a flat tyre. Told I had been up 35 minutes, it seemed like an hour and a half. Found three strikes in the machines, all in the leading edge; one of these had punctured the tyre; was amused to think that the Stukas had probably inflicted these, not one of the many 109s. Mike was back safely, but had been so harried by 109s that he hadn't seen the bombers at all.

This was my first experience of mixing it with enemy fighters, except for an inconclusive engagement with a 110 off Lowestoft last year; on the whole I'd found it encouraging: with all the advantages on their side they still hadn't shown outstanding resolution. Heard afterwards that there had been 25 Stukas and about fifteen 109s. Two Stukas had been confirmed from the ground as destroyed.

Wednesday 25.3.42
Went to Valetta with Mike to try to secure some tropical kit. Sirens sounded soon after lunch, so we made our way to the Fighter Control Room, also one of the best air-raid shelters in Valetta. There was a big raid coming in, 80 plus, against which we had managed to put six Spits and six Hurricanes. The R/T conversation was being broadcast from a loud-speaker and the breathless, staccato voices were coming through very clearly; we heard Mac say: 'There they are, five o'clock below'. Grant, who was leading, came back after slight pause: 'Can't see them, you lead, you lead'; another pause, longer this time, then Pete's voice, very excited: 'Look, Stukas, Stukas, shoals of 'em', followed by Grant's long-drawn-out, 'Geez'; another longish interval, tense and expectant, before an army telephone reported cannon-fire; another pause, then a very loud excited voice said: 'Okay, Woodie, I'm out of ammo, think I got a couple.' More chatter, then the reports from the ground began to come in: two 109s confirmed, two 87s confirmed, half a dozen

other Stukas probable or badly damaged; no losses. Clearly a pretty successful day. On return to the mess found that Mac had got one of the 109s destroyed; he was jubilant about it, more especially because he'd stolen a march on Jimmie, who only claimed a damaged Stuka.

I was rather selfishly relieved to find that the Stukas destroyed to-day died hard after taking a lot of punishment; they are supposed to be such easy meat that I'd been feeling disappointed at not having done better when I'd met them, but the general opinion now is that these are the new ones – Mark D, I think – heavily armoured and with twin dorsal guns.

III

Thursday 26.3.42

Woke up and remembered that Thursday was my lucky day and with feeling that I might get something. Came to readiness at Luqa at 1300 hours with Mike and three pilots from 249; only four aircraft serviceable, so Mike had to stand down for the first scramble. Warning went about tea-time and the four of us took off with Bud Connell leading; no Hurricanes available. Weather was perfect again; Bud headed south, climbing hard, and led us round in a wide right-handed sweep to a good position up-sun. Woodie kept us posted with a running commentary on the development of the plot: first he said ten, then twelve, finally fifteen Stukas and three 88s accompanied by the usual number of Little Boys. Heard him tell us to come in and Bud swung us north-eastward; at the same time noticed that the Grand Harbour barrage had suddenly appeared from nowhere, but couldn't see any aircraft yet. As we approached I saw two 88s break south-west out of the barrage a long way below us. The other three Spits half-rolled and went after them, I decided to wait for the Stukas; flew on till I was right over the barrage at 10,000 feet and then sat waiting for them to emerge and hoping no 109s would pick me up before they did so.

A minute or two passed and nothing happened. I began to think I must have missed them, perhaps they had gone out before the 88s. What a fool I'd been not to take that chance while I had it, now I probably wouldn't even fire my guns, and so on, when suddenly the first Stuka pulled up out of the smoke-puffs and headed north. He was a long way below me, so I had to get rid of my surplus height without gaining too much speed. I pulled throttle right back and swish-tailed down, while 87s popped up out of the barrage, one after the other, like tumblers coming up through a trap-door in the stage. There seemed so many I hardly knew which to take; was manoeuvring behind one when another overtook me and passed within 30 yards so that I could see every detail of his camouflage. The Intelligence people had thought the last lot might have been Italians, but there was no doubt about this Swastika; decided he was better target than the other, and was about to attack when he suddenly seemed to stand on his head. I tried to follow, but couldn't compete with so sudden a dive and passed over the top; as I did so I noticed his bombs leaving his belly. That was rather puzzling; I thought they'd already released all their bombs, possibly this one had shied at the barrage and chosen an easier target north of the harbour. No time for speculation; they were flying out among the big, scattered, cumulus clouds which usually build up over the island, and if I wasn't quick I should lose them. Chose the nearest and attacked dead astern with a 2-second burst of cannon and machine-guns from 150 yards; he escaped into cloud before I could see any result. Picked the next – they seemed to be on all sides – and gave him a four-second burst from 200 yards. He began to dive for a cloud, but before he reached it streams of black smoke were pouring from his belly; I followed him into it, hoping to pick him up on the other side and finish him off, but decided there was no need, so pulled up and looked for another.

Stukas were scurrying on all sides across the gaps between the clouds and I had begun to feel pleasantly like a wolf. I chose another and got in a short burst before he reached cover, but with no observed result, so looked round and found a fourth, in which I finished my machine-gun ammunition from close range; saw what looked like several jets of white vapour, spurting from round his radiator and coming back in a substantial stream; hauled off out of range of his return fire to see what would happen, and noted that the last of clouds had been left behind. Sea and sky stretched away unbroken to Sicily. Checked my gauges as a precaution and was horrified to find that the oil pressure, instead of standing at 90, was at 30 and falling as I watched. Hell! Ten or fifteen miles offshore with no ammo, and a failing engine.

I looked up again and the first thing I saw, about 300 yards ahead, flying across my bows at the same height from starboard to port, was a 109. I pulled the machine round as hard as I could – feeling like a small boy who has seen the headmaster – and headed back for the cloud-cover. Don't know why, but I had the idea that the 109 hadn't spotted me, or perhaps I thought I should reach the cloud before he could attack; anyway my head was buried in the office like an ostrich's, and I was watching the oil pressure sink to zero and busy throttling back and lowering the revs to nurse my motor, when suddenly I saw a bright flash on the top of my port wing, outboard of the cannon. I was still wondering what had happened, when the 109 overshot me and disappeared at once into the cloud ahead. I followed and was gratefully swallowed.

Called up on R/T and said: 'Emergency, emergency, my oil's gone, I may have to jump out, transmitting for fix, transmitting for fix.' Woodie came back very reassuringly and told me at once to steer 180°. I looked at the altimeter and found I had 2,500 feet, determined to hang on to this so that I should have plenty of room if I did have to bale out; undid my harness and took my gloves off, but decided to keep my helmet, so that I could still transmit. Last time my oil pressure had gone the engine had only lasted a couple of minutes before a bearing had followed, so I sat expecting that terrible juddering every moment, and wondered what I should do if the 109 found me again. At each gap in the clouds I slunk across like a branded criminal.

At last I saw the coast ahead, through a gap in the clouds, and reckoned I could almost make it; but supposing the motor failed now, which would be better, to bale out over the sea or try to crash land on the cliffs? I felt too harassed to make up my mind, and decided to leave the question open until it had to be faced. The motor still sounded sweet, but you never knew. Two minutes later I was over land and was trying to locate Takali aerodrome without exposing myself unnecessarily by leaving the clouds; couldn't see it anywhere at first, then caught sight of Musta Cathedral dome, which lies a mile to the north of it, and was heading thankfully that way, thinking that if the worst came to the worst I should be able to glide in without motor now, when Woodie came over the R/T saying: 'Look out, Pinto aircraft, 109 over Takali, 109 over Takali.' Hell, there would be, Luqa was another eight miles; was just debating whether to risk it or not, when I saw him, right ahead at the same height as myself hoped devoutly he hadn't seen me and decided to try and make Luqa.

The country underneath was hopeless for a forced landing, and I'd made up my mind not to attempt it if the motor packed up but to jump out; however skilful and lucky you were you would almost certainly write off the aircraft and probably yourself if you tried to put it down on that undulating mosaic of tiny fields and stone walls. I had the revs as low as they would go, and kept just enough boost to maintain height; the motor still sounded smooth and I began to grow hopeful. There was always that 109 though. I called up for any available Pinto aircraft to cover my landing at base, and heard Bud say Okay, okay; arrived over Luqa at last, took a furtive look round and saw no sign of the 109, came down in ordinary S turns with the throttle closed; dropped my wheels, final look round, straightened out, lowered flaps, slipped off surplus height and touched gratefully down.

The aircraft was BP 850, the one I'd flown, off the carrier. There was a machine-gun strike below the spinner which had made a jagged hole in the oil-tank, and through this most of the oil seemed to have escaped; the wing roots and belly were smothered in it. There was another strike in the spinner, which luckily had not affected the constant-speed mechanism of the air-screw, and a third in the leading edge of the starboard wing; the cannon-shell which had exploded in the port wing had blown a hole about 4 inches square through both the outer skin and the top of the main spar below it, while another cannon-shell, which I had noticed at the time, had exploded at the root of the starboard elevator and gone very near to jamming it. By and large, felt I was lucky to have got back.

Woodie was delighted: the four of us had accounted for two of the three 88s and two 87s, all of which had been confirmed from the ground, without more loss than the damage to my machine. Buck McNair got one of the 88s I'd seen him dive after. Heard later that they'd both passed over the mess, like bats out of hell, with Buck just out of range but closing perceptibly; he'd caught it very soon afterwards and set its tanks on fire. The pilot had made a successful crash-landing south of Gozo before anything exploded and the crew were picked up in their dinghy. Bud Connell had shot the tail off an 88 and then found the Stukas and finished his ammunition in them. He said he'd seen one, which must have been one of mine, going down with black smoke pouring out. The armourers found that one of my cannon had jammed after thirty rounds; pity, when I'd tested them on the *Eagle* they had both fired beautifully, without hint of a stoppage.

Friday 27.3.42
Day off flying for me; weather was poor, so little activity in the air. Spent the day putting things straight; the accounts section has now moved elsewhere and we have settled down in its place, and some beds have been found for us. Johnny Plagis and Pete Nash of 249, and Mac, Jimmie, Mike and I of 126, are sharing a room; the house is a pleasant one and looks on to a little sun-baked court, and for batmen we have three young Maltese, Charlie, Jimmie and Manuel. They seemed to spend the bulk of their time cooking their own food in the passage, and they talk incessantly, day and night, otherwise they're all right. The view from here, though less comprehensive than that from the roof of the mess, because Luqa and Halfar are less easy to see, is still very striking. It is so near Takali aerodrome that a well-driven golf-ball might almost reach the nearest of the dispersal areas. For messing purposes we are sharing with 249.

Saturday 28.3.42
Another dull day with little activity in the air. One 88 came over on reconnaissance and was intercepted by four of the 249 boys; one of them had cannon failure and didn't fire, but the other three emptied all their ammo into it and, though both engines were streaming smoke when it was last seen, it was still flying; just shows how much they'll take. Norman followed it for some time after the others had broken away, hoping for confirmation, and didn't at first notice that he'd been hit in the engine, until it began to overheat and run very roughly; he was then 25 miles out and at only 1,000 feet, so he came back in some trepidation, but made it safely.

Sunday 29.3.42
Readiness all the morning. Jimmie and I were scrambled after a lone 88, probably on reconnaissance. Sky was overcast with a single thin layer of cloud at about 10,000 feet; we climbed through this into the bright sunshine above and went up to 17,000. Woodie told us he was

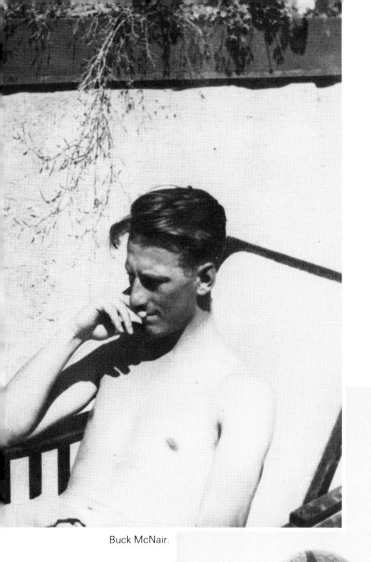

Buck McNair.

Pete Nash.

coming in from the north-east at 15,000, later that he was in our immediate vicinity, but I think he must have been in cloud all the time, because we couldn't have failed to see him against that dazzling background if he'd been in the open. Was feeling rather puzzled at missing him, when I noticed flak bursting to the south-west, and later spotted him among the puffs. He looked as if he meant to go out westwards, so waggled my wings for Jimmie to follow and set off in that direction, flat-out, hoping to cut him off and make a head-on attack as he turned for home. Kept well above him, so that we should have a background of blue sky behind us, but unfortunately we were down sun and he appeared to see us, because we saw him drop his bombs – tiny specks against the cloud – and swing away to the east. Had plenty of height and speed, so soon cut him off; came in very fast on his port beam and was about to lay sight on him when suddenly thought: 'My God, it's the Mosquito.' This had been flying earlier in the day; I'd quite forgotten about the bombs. I was coming in so fast that this momentary check spoilt the attack and I had to pull up over the top of him, cursing like hell. Watched Jimmie come in behind me, quarter astern, and saw streams of tracer flying past him as the 88 opened fire; noticed it was painted in desert camouflage. As soon as Jimmie broke away, I dived on him from above and fired until I was dead astern. Could see his tracer getting too close for comfort, so pulled up hard and then dropped a wing to watch; he was just entering cloud and a thin stream of white smoke was coming from his starboard motor. This must have been Jimmie's work, not mine, because I discovered afterwards that I had pressed the wrong button and that only my machine-guns had been fired. Was furious with myself; with so much cloud-cover I doubt whether we could have got him anyway, but I'd managed to do everything wrong and spoilt what chance we had.

All glad to see 'B' Flight arrive safely; they had been unable to take off after us last week and the Navy had sailed them back to Gib. They would have had an easier trip if they had followed us, because the weather at the second attempt had been indifferent and they had been forced to fly on the deck most of the way. Some claim they saw about thirty CR 42s on patrol near Pantellaria; sounds improbable, but may be true. Seven new Spits will be useful. Indications are that

(*Right*) Laddie Lucas
(*Below*) Norman MacQueen
and Johnny Plagis.

in Sicily the Hun has about 200 Ju 88s, 40 Stukas, 120 Me 109s, and a number of odds and ends, over 400 in all.

Monday 30.3.42
Day off flying. Dislike being on one day and off the next, would much rather put up with twice the intensity for half as long; as it is, work myself up one day only to run down again in the interval, so that next time the process has to be gone through again. Think it is the same with most people, but there are a few who seem able to change their mood at will; wish I could. We all had to go down to the aerodrome to help build blast-pens for the aircraft which are supposed to be on their way; literally dozens are being constructed and everyone has to help, Maltese workmen, the Army and ourselves. Spent the morning with pick and shovel and rather enjoyed it. Walked back to the mess and was told no beer to be had; local brewery has virtually closed down for lack of barley and they haven't been able to import any for months, so suppose it can't be helped. Usual Maconochie for lunch.

Tuesday 31.3.42
Went on readiness in the afternoon; didn't feel at all ambitious after lunch, but gradually screwed myself up until, by dusk, was sorry that nothing had turned up. At 7.30 they released us; went out to the aircraft to fetch my kit and had no sooner got back to the dispersal-hut, about five or seven minutes later, when told over the phone to take cover; asked whether we could take off, but was told no. Wing Commander Turner arrived; said plot was very big one and we'd better come underground, he thought the raid would be directed at the aerodrome. We asked him whether we couldn't go up after them and he almost relented – think he was rather keen to come with us – but found that all the crews had disappeared so decided it was too late.

Almost dark by now; we all stood in the mouth of 'G' shelter and watched. Four Hurricanes had taken off and they climbed up and disappeared, then the searchlights came on, one after the other, until the sky was full of their beams, and finally the ack-ack opened up. The raiders didn't seem to be coming in from any particular direction. One came in from the south and was at once picked up by the searchlights; it was a Ju 88, and we could see it writhing about as it tried to throw the beams off, but they never looked like losing him, and he was in the end forced to turn out to sea again. Half a dozen Bofors guns opened up at him, and it was fascinating to watch the converging streams of their fire, the tracers showing up a most vivid red against the dark background; they seemed so picturesque and unhurried that they might have been red ping-pong balls. The raid didn't develop on the aerodrome after all, most of the bombs seemed to fall in the Grand Harbour area; heard later the Hurricanes got a probable.

Wednesday 1.4.42
Spent the morning working on the pen we are building; perfect day, with bright sun and fresh wind blowing from the north-west. The island had its best yet and bagged fourteen, four for the guns and ten for the fighters. These all fell to 249 without loss to themselves; three 109s, two 88s, five 87s. Johnny Plagis made four trips and got one each time; Pete Nash secured a couple that must have given him some satisfaction: an 88 hit in the petrol-tanks which flicked over on to its back and spun down into the sea, and an 87 which more or less disintegrated as he closed in on it. Wish mine would do something dramatic like that instead of dying so hard. I may be doing something wrong; if only we had camera guns I could tell. The Spits made an extraordinary good job of the last raid; five of them were found and attacked by 15-20 109s before the Stukas came in, but they stuck together and kept their ammo. Each time the 109s came down they turned in to them at the right moment, mixed it, and afterwards reformed. When the 87s finally arrived, they managed to shake off the attentions of the Little Boys and get themselves a Stuka apiece. Convinced that these are the right tactics; the plan by which the Spits provide high cover for a handful of Hurricanes is waste of aircraft.

Discussed again the question of invasion, one we think about a good deal. None of us can make up his mind on the subject: there are so many reasons why he should, and so many why he shouldn't attempt it. The majority of the prisoners of war think it will come, on the argument that they cannot again afford to allow us to become a thorn in Rommel's flesh, and that their losses in taking the island would probably be smaller, in the long run, than the losses in convoy and in Africa if it were left in our possession. Against this the other school argues that, with only a few places where landings from the sea are possible, a heavy concentration of ack-ack and some fighters, we should probably be a much stiffer fence than Crete and should be able to inflict prohibitive losses; further that Malta is too rocky, and the fields too small, to allow even gliders to land. This their opponents won't allow: there were scores of places where any type of glider could crash-land without too much damage to the occupants; moreover, this time the Navy would be able to offer no help at all. Finally had they realised how much the strength of Malta was compromised by the proximity of Gozo? If the Huns took one, the other was doomed. I believed that if the enemy was prepared to pay a very heavy price he might take the island; everything in the war had shown that, if he regarded an objective as essential, he didn't consider expense, so the problem resolved itself into one of trying to guess Hitler's plans for 1942 and to gauge the importance to them of Malta. The attention we had received from the Luftwaffe showed that something impressive was being prepared in Africa, and this implied that ultimate invasion was a probability; on the other hand, if Rommel were completely successful and reached Suez there could be no need to invade, we should fall into his lap. I couldn't get further than this. If Ju 52s had been reported one day in Sicily, no one would have been surprised; until then I suppose we shall all go on hoping for the best.

IV

Thursday 2.4.42

Remembered it was the day before Good Friday and therefore, in a way, the anniversary of my first combat. Came to readiness at Luqa at dawn with Mac, Jimmie, Canada, Chris and Australia. Heard that a big raid was coming in; at 0930 we were scrambled, four Spits and two Hurricanes. Strapped myself into the aircraft, put my helmet on, and pressed the starter button; nothing happened. I thought the battery must be dead, so told the crew to bring another, tried again, but still no response. Mac already had his engine running, so I shouted to him to lead and I would join them later if I could. Took myself and my kit out and drove across to another bay, where there was supposed to be a serviceable aircraft, started up and got away about three minutes behind the others.

There was a thin layer of cloud at 2,000 feet, and by the time they had broken through this and joined up with the two Hurricanes I'd caught them. Was debating whether to take over the lead, when I discovered that the R/T transmission was dud, so decided to let Mac carry on and took up position on extreme left. The six of us climbed in right-hand spirals to 15,000 feet over the island, then headed eastwards out to sea, still climbing, until we reached a position about eight miles off-shore at 21,000 feet. Woodie told us that the bandits were 30 miles north-east of the island at 14,000 feet, and the Little Jobs, at the same height, were sweeping in ahead of them. We circled that position, when I saw the two Hurricanes fly off at a tangent to the north-east. Mac didn't seem to have noticed so I called him on the R/T, but of course he couldn't hear. Woodie gave the position of the bandits again, still 30 miles away; that seemed ominous, it looked as if they were hanging about until the 109s had found and engaged us.

It was a lovely morning. The sun seemed very bright already,

57

although it was still quite early; perhaps the light was intensified by the dazzling cloud-carpet miles below. Four Spits continued to orbit. I noticed a couple of 109s far away to the north at about the same height; as I watched they seemed to climb and were lost to view; another pair appeared to the west, much closer. I warned the others, in case any of them could hear me, but no one seemed to. All four of us were weaving now, rather too much for coherence, I thought, and when on the outside I had to be very careful not to get left behind on the turns. Began to feel most uncomfortable: where were those bloody bombers? Had been looking all round me and, except for those two pairs of 109s in the distance, had seen nothing at all. Then suddenly there was a 109 diving in on my port quarter, quite close and already firing. We were in a left-hand turn and I was on the inside, with the other three banked up rather above me, so I wrenched the aircraft round as tight as it would go and kicked on full bottom rudder; called to them to break left and saw that Jimmie, who was next to me, already had his nose well down and seemed to have seen the danger, but the other two were flying normally; as I watched, one of them became suddenly enveloped in smoke and flame, seemed to stall, and fell away into a spin. Quickly glanced back over my left shoulder and saw what looked like ten or twelve 109s above, some diving on us, others apparently waiting their turn; they were quite close, and they appeared to be jet black, so that they hardly showed up at all against the intensely blue sky, except occasionally where the sun caught a perspex hood.

It was a sinister sight. Impressions of the next few minutes are jumbled and blurred: can remember being attacked by a number of 109s, some of which fired and some of which didn't; remember noticing one which was trying to creep up on me from underneath, turning in to him head-on and seeing him flash past within a few yards; remember seeing an aircraft flying westwards with a long plume of glycol streaming behind him; remember noting the yellow nose on another 109 which passed very close; finally remember spotting the barrage miles below and feeling thankful that the bombers had at last arrived and I could go down and have a bang at them. Did a half-roll and such fierce aileron turns that I was partially blacked out; the aircraft kept trying to pull out and climb, and the stick was so heavy that in the end I had to correct the tendency on the tail-trim. Pulled out and took a careful look all round: alone, thank goodness; realised then for the first time how terribly tired I was.

Flew towards the barrage, slightly downhill, weaving gently and keeping a look-out behind and above all the time; picked out some 88s among the bursts, they were well above cloud and must have been bombing through it. Thought at first they were going out westward, away from me, until the first one had almost passed; even then it did not occur to me until afterwards that I'd missed a chance of delivering head-on attacks on the whole bunch of them. Instead I did a stall-turn and dived after the nearest one. Opened fire from astern and above, with machine-guns at 300 yards; closed to 100 yards, firing short, savage bursts until my cannon ammunition was exhausted. At first I had seen no results, but later there had been a large flash and an impression of smoke from his starboard motor; noticed no return fire. Pulled up out of range, and then dropped a wing to have a look; was almost directly above him and expected to see some kind of damage, but there was nothing, no fire, no smoke, no glycol, only noticed that his props were turning very slowly, but this might have been bravado, not injury. Didn't approve in theory of the attack I'd made, firing everything into his armour, but I'd known I shouldn't be left alone long enough to attempt anything artistic.

No time for disappointment, immediately found myself attacked by a 109. Avoided him, but as I did so, my scarf, which had been working looser and looser ever since I changed machines on the ground, came completely undone and almost flew out of the cockpit; grabbed it in time and began to wedge it under my seat; one part of me thought: 'You are a b. f., something is sure to get you while you're playing about like this,' but the other stubbornly said: 'I'm blowed if these little buzzards are going to make me lose B's scarf.'

As soon as it was firmly stowed I looked back behind me, and sure enough there was a 109 sitting on my tail, firing. As I evaded him another flew across in front of me and began a left-hand climbing turn, offering a lovely shot. I'd just pushed my bead out in front of him, when I saw something in the corner of my right eye; still don't know whether it was a burst of flak or a 109, but I wasn't taking any more chances and half-rolled down to cloud-cover. Knew there was some machine-gun ammunition left, and felt I should go up again and have a bang at something else, but found myself terribly reluctant to do so; problem was solved when I checked my gauges, oil pressure was down to zero again. Broke down below cloud and found myself a mile or two south-east of Luqa. Didn't know how long my motor would last, so cut the throttle, did a tight right-hand half-circuit and dropped on to the long runway.

No trace of any of the others: that looked bad. Phoned Fighter Control and was told that someone, they thought Mac, was in a dinghy three miles east of Calafrana; the rescue launch was already on its way, but would need an escort. I arranged for Australia and Chris to go with it; a rumour had already come through that 109s were shooting the dinghy up, but this was unconfirmed. When they'd gone another machine landed, this proved to be Jimmie. He had seen the 109s at about the same time and had broken with me; he reckoned there were fifteen of them, but hadn't been hit; he'd heard Mac say that he was baling out east of Calafrana and had gone there to search for him, but without success. Later Australia and Chris returned and reported they had seen someone picked up by the rescue boat off Calafrana, and this proved to be Mac, slightly wounded. Nothing had been heard of Canada, so Australia and Chris set off again to make a sea-search, but found no trace. Conditions were ideal and both were sure they couldn't have missed him if he'd been out there in his dinghy; it looked as if his was the aircraft I'd seen hit and he'd been unable to get out.

Went out to look at my machine, feeling terribly tired and dispirited. The fuselage was smothered in oil and I counted more than 20 holes, some made by machine guns and some by cannon. An oil pipe in the port wing root had been severed by a slug that came in from astern; that was probably the work of the 109 which had jumped me when I was fumbling with the scarf. A cannon shell had passed horizontally through the fuselage from port to starboard five feet behind my seat, and two others had hit the rudder and starboard elevator; these three were beam shots and were probably inflicted in the first attack. I was glad to see that the shot which damaged the oil-system was the only one to enter from astern: at any rate I hadn't made it easier for them. When we'd been getting away with it, we'd found the odds against us rather exhilarating, but now we had suffered our first losses the prospect had suddenly become depressing. On the first day the weather had been so bad that the enemy aircraft had operated in a stream, but singly; since then we'd been two against 40, four against 30 plus, and six against 35 plus.

Went to Calafrana at lunch time; the water was like a mirror. Found Mac in the underground sick quarters with shrapnel in leg and arm, but astonishingly cheerful. He said he had just sighted the bombers when he was hit, had never heard Jimmie or me say break left, and had never seen what got him. His left leg had gone quite numb at once so that he had to use his right foot on both sides of the rudder; his arm was also hit but remained serviceable. The actuating gear seemed to have been shot away, because he had to hold the stick fully forward with all his strength to maintain a slight dive; his port aileron had been knocked almost upright, and the only evasive action he had dared to take was a gentle turn in one direction and a skid in the oher. He had headed west and hoped to get the machine home, but had been followed by 109s all the way down, had counted six attacks in all; the starboard side of the instrument panel had been shot away, his R/T had been shot away, and he had had to cower behind his armour-plating and listen to the bullets rattling against it. The machine I'd seen flying west with its glycol streaming out had probably been his, but he didn't know about that and had thought his motor was all right.

Before his R/T had been taken from him, he had apparently talked incessantly; I'd been too busy myself to notice, but Jimmie heard it all. First he'd said 'Hullo, Gondar, Red Leader here, think I've been hit, but trying to make base'; later, 'Hello, Wombat aircraft, go down after the big jobs, I've got all the Little Boys playing with me'; then, 'Think I can make it, but if I don't Good Huntin' fellers'; finally, 'Hello, Jimmie, going down in the drink just east Calafrana.' At cloud level the machine had begun to burn and he had prepared to jump out; then the elevator wires had snapped and the aircraft had flipped up on its back, making it rather difficult for him to get out, but he had got clear in his parachute and hit the water close behind his machine. At first he'd been unable to get rid of his harness, because the R/T cable caught in the release-buckle. By this time he was almost exhausted and thought he would drown, remembered saying to himself 'Godammit, Mac, this is the hell of a way to get killed', but had then managed to free himself, inflate his dinghy and crawl into it. Soon afterwards a strange aircraft had flown low overhead, silver all over with a small black cross, neither 109 nor Macchi 202. It had begun to circle and he thought it was aiming to shoot him up, so he jumped out into the sea and hid behind the dinghy; it had come back, but hadn't fired. After what seemed like an hour to an hour and a half – actually twenty to twenty-five minutes – the rescue launch had arrived and picked him up.

We took Mac back to the mess with us, somewhat bizarrely dressed. This had been our first loss; the arithmetic suffered but was still quite good: seven destroyed and some probable, for the loss of one pilot killed and one slightly wounded. Poor Canada, he never even had a shot at them.

Don't like the way the number of hits that I receive is increasing. The first time it was two strikes, the next time three, then five, now 20 something – there's no future in it.

Friday 3.4.42
Aircraft situation so bad that both squadrons had to be released so that serviceability could be improved. Idle day, nothing to do. A number of new pilots joined the squadron: Tex, whom I'd known in 133; Brooker, an experienced Canadian; Goldsmith, an Australian; Schade, of Malaya; and Jemmet, an Englishman. Tex and Goldie had been here on Hurricanes and knew the island, but the other three were new to it.

Rumours everywhere that the mess is going to be blitzed; said to have been given out on the Rome radio and no doubt disseminated by the local Fifth Column. Civilians more jumpy than usual, pilots too, for that matter. Heavy gun-fire at tea-time, then bombs shaking the building; everyone rushed outside. Mac and I headed for the air-raid shelter near the bridge over the moat, Mac making wonderful time in spite of his gammy leg; felt rather shamefaced on arrival, so stayed outside to watch.

Often wondered what the Maltese thought at seeing so many pilots on the ground during raids: one was heard to say that he couldn't understand why we had to rely on the barrage when there

(*Right*) Patrick Schade.

(*Below*) Soldiers and sailors refuelling a Spitfire of 126 Squadron.

were 150 Spits ready to take off; another – an omniscient small boy – that we had only eight aircraft left. It would be understandable if they showed some surliness when they saw us on the ground and not in the air, and it's to their credit that they never do; they seem to realise that it isn't our fault if we aren't flying, and although we can do little enough – and what we do shoot down is usually out of their sight – they still retain a pathetic belief in us.

First raid appeared to be a false alarm, but later more gun-fire brought us out on the roof. There were 21 Stukas at about 14,000 feet in a long straggling crocodile working round to the south. When they were almost overhead the leading pair put their noses down and headed straight for us; possibly it was intentional, for after all those rumours everyone thought we would be the objective. Jimmie and Australia both bolted for the stairs, but I thought it was too late to start running for cover, and in any case am rather claustrophobic, so determined to stay on the roof where I was. Very unpleasant moment before the two Stukas straightened their dives and headed for the aerodrome. Down they came through terrific barrage, one behind the other, each let three bombs go at about 4,000 feet, then achieved an astonishingly tight pull-out, which is supposed to be automatic and not controlled by the pilot, and climbed steeply – weaving hard all the time – to 5-6,000 feet.

Both the Bofors guns on this side of the aerodrome were firing like blazes; sometimes it would seem as if one of their red billiard-balls must hit the aircraft, but at the last moment it would veer to one side and the shell would overtake it, apparently quite slowly, and burst with a jerk, as if on the end of a string, in a grey puff. Their objective was clearly dispersed aircraft, and the bombing was good. The first stick fell just inside the southern perimeter, the second just outside it; a great pall of dust rose up and all the remaining bombs disappeared into it, you couldn't even see the bursts, the dust just rose higher and grew thicker. I crouched behind the balustrade and watched, wishing I had either a Spit or a camera; some of the Stukas might have been hit by the flak, but none fell, and as soon as they were out of range they reformed in an untidy gaggle and flew away northward. There were no 109s to be seen, they seem to know when we're grounded. When it was all over, the other two appeared again: Australia rather sheepishly because he has been pooh-poohing bombing, Jimmie still nervous as a cat and not ashamed of it.

Single raiders came over all night; I twice heard the whine of a diving engine and dashed outside, thinking the blitz had begun, but each time it was a false alarm. Mac was so determined not to be caught that he came out in his pyjamas, barefooted. I don't like the idea of being caught in one of these Maltese houses; with floors and ceiling of soft stone they would be death-traps.

Saturday 4.4.42
Another day off, so Old Bailey arranged a tour of the Rabat catacombs. A wonderful ruffian of a guide showed us round with what we thought was surprising learning; discovered later that it all came out of a book which he offered me as a favour at 10/−, and which I later bought in Valetta for 6/6. His main delight was in his skeletons and in sneering at the theories of the rival catacomb-keeper across the way. Dutifully we sneered too.

Ever since he got shot down Mac has been threatening to get drunk, apparently on the principle that to do so would exorcise his memories; carried out his threat to-day in a lunch-time session.

Sunday 5.4.42
Mac woke up remembering nothing, but with a head and tongue that told their story. He wouldn't admit it, at first, and tried to bluff us with some Macleod bluster; we were ready for him, though, and said it was too bad about that Spit, but he had only himself to blame. What Spit? Mac asked. Why, surely he remembered what had happened? No, he didn't remember anything about a Spit. What, didn't he even remember taking a swing at an airman who had tried to keep him out of it? No, he didn't think he remembered that either. Well, if that had been all, it wouldn't have mattered much, but when we were so short of aircraft, to go and ... Well, I'll be a sad son-of-a-bitch, Mac said, did I go and break an aircraft? What, did he mean to say he'd no recollection of the bomb-hole? Yes, slap into it. No, not very much damage, an oleo-leg and a wing-tip, and of course the airscrew. By the way, the Wing-Co had left a message that he would see Mac at 10 o'clock.

By this time the bluster had evaporated and Mac was looking

pretty chastened. The story had been well canvassed and it wasn't until after breakfast that Mac was able to establish his innocence ; even then he had to put up with some· pointed homilies from Jimmie.

Came to readiness in the afternoon with Tex, Australia and Dusty. When we were scrambled Dusty's machine went unserviceable and he had to land; I led the other two south and we climbed in a wide-right-handed sweep which brought us back over Gozo at 10,000 feet. Raiders hadn't appeared yet; we turned east and headed for Grand Harbour so as to be at hand when they arrived. Saw some 109s in the distance, then four aircraft flew overhead; thought at first they were more 109s, but they proved to be Hurricanes. After experience last Thursday decided it would pay better not to climb too high, but to stay in the intermediate levels, so flattened out at about 11,000 feet and began to orbit. Seemed to be a great number of aircraft about, but nothing molested us; learnt afterwards there had been 83 bombers and about 50 fighters. Heard Gondar say something about fighter-bombers, and then at the critical moment the R/T went unserviceable. Looked down and saw bomb-bursts on the ground; clearly something had come in without our spotting it, so waggled my wings and went down in spirals to see what it was. Saw nothing at first, then picked out two 109s below me; dived on the nearer one and waited until I had closed right in to 100 yards before giving him a short burst, which immediately produced a large puff of grey smoke in the neighbourhood of his exhaust manifolds: that was much more satisfactory. Took a precautionary look behind and seeing something above me, broke violently and unnecessarily away to starboard and in doing so lost my quarry.

Tex and Australia had disappeared; decided to try and regain my height. As I was doing so I noticed 88s above me diving on Grand Harbour from the north-west; at the same time the barrage opened up again. Realised that I should be too late and too low to catch the leaders, so flew round to the south, flat-out and still climbing hard, in the hope of picking up one of the stragglers.

We'd noticed that the close escort· left the bombers before they entered the barrage; our tactics, therefore, were to deliver our attacks during the period when the bombers had been dropped by the close escort and before they had been picked up again by the patrols waiting offshore. Sometimes it meant following them through the barrage, but everyone agreed that this was preferable to the 109s; you at least felt that the barrage was friendly at heart, but the Little Boys never succeeded in conveying that impression. The new bursts were black and hard-looking, but gradually they expanded and grew grey and fluffy; the barrage was heavy to-day and you felt you were flying round something tangible – it made me think of a giant chestnut-tree in flower.

As I was waiting for suitable target, I looked up and saw eight or ten 109s in ragged line astern, flying north; they didn't seem to notice me, thank goodness. Next moment spotted an 88 pulling out of its dive and heading north-east; chased it flat-out and at first seemed to make no impression whatever; remembered I'd been climbing, he diving, so hung on and gradually the range began to close. It had almost done so when I saw two 109s of the protective cordon heading towards me; knew it was useless to go on, since they had clearly spotted me, therefore turned toward them and both went past without firing. But another, which I hadn't seen at all, came diving out of the sun at me almost head-on; as I saw him open fire I pushed the stick forward hard and saw a torrent of tracer fly over my head. Imagine the Huns must have tracers at every tenth round; as the aircraft flies over the old tracers you can watch new ones appearing in their place – they don't form or grow, they simply appear. Often the new ones seem to be slightly out of line with the old – probably because an aircraft at high speed is an unstable firing platform – and are more sharply defined in colour and outline. Sometimes seeing an aircraft open fire gives the impression that it has suddenly shot its tentacles out at you, or that it has grown some curious light-blue antennae since last you looked; occasionally the eye is quick enough to follow the making of a trace, and then it may seem a little frightening because of its speed, but normally they are not sinister for what they appear, but what they are.

Having avoided this 109 I saw a Stuka climbing out of the barrage towards me; headed for him and prepared to attack, when more 109s appeared from nowhere and rode me off; didn't see any of them firing, but I was forced to lose height to evade them, and lost the Stuka too. Flew in over Grand Harbour; everything seemed to have disappeared, until I picked out a lone 88 going north; began to chase him, but he had altitude and I realised that I should never catch him this side of Sicily, so gave it up. For first time I'd failed to fire at a bomber.

Reached Takali and entered the circuit warily. Took a good look round before dropping my wheels and noticed two aircraft above and behind me. I'd just decided they were Hurricanes when I noticed red tracer flying all round them; I whipped round so fast I almost spun and they both passed overhead; heard afterwards they were 109s and had fired a quick, wild burst at me. That was the second time I'd almost been jumped on the circuit; still find it difficult to be as vigilant there as one should be. Landed and found that both Tex and Australia had got back safely, though Australia had been shot up and had had to land with his wheels up; he had splinter wounds and had been taken off to hospital. He had shot down a Stuka and claimed an 88 probably destroyed as well; this was confirmed later. Tex had secured an 88 destroyed and I claimed my 109, after hearing that a single parachute had appeared some miles off-shore, as a probable; moreover for the first time from a big raid I'd brought my machine back unscathed.

We went to see Australia in the evening and found him two beds away from a 109 pilot called Kurt whom MacQueen had shot down a couple of weeks earlier. Australia was very cheerful in spite of a good deal of shrapnel in his legs. He said he had a good bang at an 88 which he reckoned to have destroyed, finished his cannon in another without apparent result, and finally had a long chase after a Stuka which took him farther out to sea than he'd intended. He'd given it all his remaining machine-gun ammunition and it had fallen away in a spiral dive, smoking hard; at the same moment he'd looked up and seen two 109s above him, had dived for the deck, thinking to trace them home, but had been caught in no time and had been subjected to a series of scientific attacks from both quarters. One cannon shell had burst in the bottom of the cockpit and wounded him, another in front of his face without injuring him. He'd roared in on the deck through Grand Harbour, thinking this would throw them off, but they had followed him all the way to Takali, then transferred their attentions to me. When first hit, he thought his whole leg had been shot away, as it had gone quite numb. He told us that Kurt had laughed like a drain when he'd been brought in, so as we left he called after us 'Good luck, chaps, and get lots more, you'll find the 109s are easiest.' Kurt grinned and stroked his chin.

Monday 6.4.42
Spent the whole morning working on our blast-pen, it was cool enough to be pleasant. The Maltese workmen on the aerodrome not only have their wages doubled for war-risks, but have a fleet of buses standing by all the time to bear them away to the shelters as soon as the siren sounds; we don't grudge them the money, but we do grudge the transport, as we have the greatest difficulty in getting even a car to take us to readiness or to move our kit out to the very widely dispersed aircraft. This morning nothing came near the aerodrome, but there was one small raid on the eastern end of the island and a number of reccos; the result was the workmen were whisked away about ten o'clock and didn't reappear until nearly half-past twelve. However, they are quite friendly and if the warning sounds at the right time we get lifts up the hill with them. They retain a pathetic faith, and one embarrassed Pete the other day by trying to kiss his hand; the younger Maltese always greets us with 'Hello, Pilots'.

V

Tuesday 7.4.42

Got up early for dawn readiness, only to find that there were no aircraft serviceable and that someone was supposed to have told us that we had been released. Mike and I walked on to the Bastion to see the dawn; looking seaward from there somehow reminded one of the scene in *Othello* when the good gentlemen of Cyprus are wondering where the Turk is and what he's up to. Away to the north we could see the Sicilian coast and Etna, not an off-white cone as usual, but in silhouette against the pale sky behind. It was a lovely morning.

Later Mike and I went to Valetta to do some shopping and have a good lunch. We'd hardly finished when the sirens sounded; decided the best thing to do would be to go to Fighter Control, we should just be able to make it before the first bombers appeared. We arrived at the entrance thinking we'd timed it nicely – the first guns were opening up – only to find that it was completely blocked by a collapsed house. We knew a back way, but it was much too far, so we had to choose between a shelter and a gun-site; chose the gun-site. It was deserted, and the Bofors had been dismantled, but the sandbags seemed reassuring and the position overlooked the whole of Grand Harbour from a small spur and we thought we'd chosen rather well.

The first wave was all 88s and they dropped their bombs across the harbour in the dockyard area; a heavy barrage was put up and occasionally we could hear the shrapnel falling; began to wish I had a tin hat. After slight pause the second wave arrived; they were Stukas, and flew almost directly overhead before beginning to dive, then came down much more steeply than the 88s and pulled out lower. The target seemed to be the *Penelope* on the other side of the harbour; we crouched behind our sandbags and saw bombs fall all round her, but nothing appeared to hit, while she shot back at them with every gun, a most inspiring sight.

The huge pall of dust and smoke which the bombs had raised on the other side gradually drifted over until the sky was hidden; with it came the third wave and this time the target was Valetta, our side of the harbour. I found it really frightening, because we could see nothing and there was nothing we could do. Above the racket of the barrage we would hear the scream of a diving motor, the whistle of the bombs, the thud and concussion of the explosion. Sometimes the whistle was long, and we'd know the bomb would fall some distance away, sometimes it was short and very sudden and we'd know it was a near one. The shortest of all ended in a stupendous explosion behind us, followed by a shower of dust and small pieces of masonry; near the gun-mounting, about six feet away from us, a fairly large block of stone appeared without either of us having heard or noticed its arrival.

I lay on the ground and thought of the graveyard passage in *All Quiet* and wondered whether this was as bad as the shelling of the last war; they say it isn't. Fear is a curious thing; I was definitely frightened, I could feel my heart thudding and would find myself shrinking at each whistle, things that I'd never experienced in the air. To keep up appearances I grimaced at Mike and he returned it. Told myself that I wasn't going to be killed in an air-raid, but wished heartily it would end. At last it did; heard afterwards that it was the largest raid that Malta had had until then, 104 bombers. We went and had a drink, shampoo and tea. The barber asked us why we didn't bomb Rome, which is a favourite demand with the Maltese; I told him that 300 bombers had just been over the Ruhr. That's all very well, he argued, but these come from Sicily; I pointed out that they were German bombers for all that; yes, but it's the Italians who brought them here, he said. Most of the Maltese seem to feel the same way, the Germans mean nothing to them, but they know and understand the Italians and are therefore doubly mad with them for bringing the war to the Mediterranean. Had hardly finished tea when the alert sounded again; it was difficult to believe that they could mount another big raid again so soon, but we weren't taking any chances and waited near the shelter in Palace Square. Walking round the Square we noticed the stone eagle outside the garrison library: its head was slewed right round so that it was watching its own tail; wise bird, we thought, clearly brought up in a good squadron; it would make a good emblem for the Malta Wing.

The first of the 88s came in from the south-east and seemed to be very high. Mike and I went down to the shelter, which must have been 35 feet deep, and stood at the foot of the steps. We could hear the guns firing and then without any warning there was a tremendous bang, followed by darkness; thought at first that the mouth of the shelter had been hit, because the blast-wave had been very heavy, but two soldiers came stumbling down the steps, smothered in white dust and badly shaken, said it had caught them outside and bowled them over. Was impressed with the way the Maltese accepted the bombing: the older people all appeared quite phlegmatic and talked of their chores and shopping, the small boys seemed to find it exciting and rather enjoyable, only a girl opposite us began to cry when the raid was at its height. We smiled reassuringly and said something trivial which seemed to comfort her; I suppose she thought that as we were in uniform we knew.

The all clear sounded at about 7 p.m. We found the bomb which had shaken us so much had fallen fully 80 yards away in front of the Public Library, making an immense crater; forgot to notice how Queen Victoria had taken it, must remember to look next time. Strada Reale was a shambles; there seemed to be almost as much new damage as old from all the previous raids, and it was clear that this time the town, not the docks, had been the objective. Every few yards there were obstructions where houses had collapsed across the street. The Opera House had received a direct hit and half of it had been demolished – no great loss, perhaps, architecturally; the Castile had been damaged and outside the city hardly a bus seemed to have escaped. The rock shelters are so effective that we only saw a single stretcher-case; the ARP people were behaving extremely well, but some of the other civilians seemed rattled. The local stone is so soft that houses collapse easily; even when the walls stand, the floors commonly fall through; mercifully there is little wood in their construction and they never seem to burn.

We decided it would appear bad and possibly give false impressions if we tried to secure any transport, so we set out to walk back. Floriana and Ham Run were both heavily damaged. Felt very gloomy, both the last raids had obviously been directed at civilian morale; there had been rumours that Berlin had announced that since Malta was impregnable to invasion by sea or air, their only remaining course was to bomb us out, and it began to appear that the new policy had started. With so few aircraft, I couldn't see what we could do to stop it; the only possible answer as things were now would be the threat of reprisals on, say, Cologne. Felt very strongly that we ought to defend our outposts better: when war broke out there were three Gladiators in the island, Faith, Hope, and Charity. Admittedly the Huns still have the initiative and move on interior lines, and I suppose this makes all the difference in the world. Told myself I ought to be angry or defiant, but found myself numb and depressed: both these raids had been 150 plus, what could we do against such numbers with four Spits and a couple of Hurricanes? Both glad to get away from Valetta; had begun to feel we were witnessing the beginning of a Warsaw or Rotterdam.

Wednesday 8.4.42

A day of raids; four Spits and some Hurricanes took off against the afternoon wave and we congregated on the roof of the mess to watch. We saw the 88s diving through the barrage over Grand Harbour and right on the tail of one of them a Spit; saw the Spit checked in its tracks as if it had been hit, and then dive straight on into the ground without ever looking as if it could pull out. No one had seen the pilot get out and we wondered rather gloomily who it was, but later the news came through that it was Nippy Heppell and that he had baled out safely. All sorts of theories about what hit him, ack-ack, a canister thrown by the 88, but it was established later that it was a direct hit from a Bofors firing at the 88 ahead of him.

At dusk three Spits took off to attack the Huns just offshore; they found a big Dornier flying-boat on the water with an escort of two 88s and about a dozen 109s and waded straight into them. Ron West saw the Dornier had ordinary camouflage and black, not red, crosses; it rather foolishly opened fire on him with a cannon, so he attacked it with a short burst and it at once exploded. From the roof of the mess we could see it burning furiously on the sea. He then went on to shoot down one of the 109s from the half dozen which attacked him, and Kelly claimed one of the 88s; all this occupied about five minutes, nice work for three Spits, one of which had cannon failure. Wonder what the leader of the 109 escort is going to say when he reaches home minus the flying-boat, an 88, and a 109, with nothing to show for it.

Germans always like to have these things both ways: if their pilots machine-gun refugees it is total war; if the refugees retaliate by bumping the pilots off, it is monstrous barbarity and ten Frenchmen will suffer for every innocent German. The 109s have put up some black shows here: the Gozo boat is regularly machine-gunned, the rescue-launch has been badly shot-up on a number of occasions, the whole crew being killed or wounded on one of them, and a 249 pilot who baled out is said to have been killed because a 109 flew over his parachute and collapsed it with his slipstream. Must admit I never met anyone who vouched for the last incident at first-hand.

Thursday 9.4.42
Heard rumour that Huns sent over another flying-boat with an escort of 120 109s; obviously untrue, but a good story, especially as not a single Spit was serviceable at that time. Most people seem to think that a reprisal raid on us is possible.

Goldie and I got caught half-way to the aerodrome by the evening raid, so took shelter at the Bofors site, where we arrived just in time. Two waves of twelve 88s attacked Takali flying towards us; the first lot appeared to aim at the northern dispersal area, but all their bombs missed and landed in Musta. Heard later that two of them had hit the Cathedral, but both had failed to explode; the Maltese believe it to be invulnerable, but I don't know whether this was divine intervention or delayed action. The second wave aimed much better and dropped everything in the southern dispersal area, almost at our feet. Bofors crew were magnificent; Goldie and I retired into their cubbyhole when we saw the bombs on the way, but they kept firing at the 88s without a break as these went overhead. After the raid we went down to the aerodrome and inspected the craters; there were two very big ones. Total casualties were only one member of a Lewis gun's crew killed and two unserviceable aircraft further damaged. No machines available, so no readiness after all.

Friday 10.4.42

Another morning with pick and shovel and another afternoon off. The third raid of the day developed, as usual, at about 5 p.m.; went out on the Bastion and saw four Spits and twelve Hurricanes take off, almost the fighter-umbrella the Hun is said to mention in his bulletins. The 109s began to come in in their usual pairs and fours, and it wasn't long before a number of dog-fights had developed at 12-15,000 feet; found it very difficult to distinguish friendly from hostile aircraft at this range. One machine was hit, a trail of black smoke appeared behind him and he fell off in a right-hand spiral dive, which gradually became steeper and steeper; at the last moment it looked as if he might recover, until we realised he was past vertical and on his back; he hit the ground north-east of Musta in a great burst of flame. Thought at the time that it was a Spit, but it later proved be a Hurricane. No one had seen the pilot bale out, but a chute had miraculously appeared; there was some anxiety that the 109s might find him and shoot him up, but none did and he finally fell among the houses in Nashar. He'd hardly landed when someone said, 'Look, a flamer'. Over Halfar a ball of fire was falling in what seemed to be the most leisurely way; again no one saw the pilot bale out, but a solitary chute appeared.

Mac and Geoff West agreed that the first one to run for a shelter should buy the other a beer, but when a wave of 88s, which no one had noticed in the general excitement, appeared almost overhead they cancelled the bet by mutual agreement and only one man reached the shelter before Mac. We had watched him before, he was a priest. At the first sign of imminent danger he would not stampede; while the others drew ahead he would pause to cram his beaver over his eyebrows, pick up his skirts from ankle to hip and then, setting off at an astonishing pace with a high-kneed action, he would outstrip the whole field and always win. Mac called him the midnight express, and acknowledged his mastery.

These 88s bombed Takali; one of them was hit and three men appeared to bale out, though only one chute opened. Learnt later that it was two men and part of the aircraft; the rear-gunner and most of his gun-position had been blown off the rest of the machine and had fallen on the aerodrome; Johnny Plagis, who inspected the body, said he wasn't wearing a chute or harness. The 88 crashed farther on; it was at first attributed to the ack-ack, but later claimed by Norman, who appeared that night wearing the dead gunner's cap. When the bombers had all disappeared a mass of 109s remained behind to attack the Hurricanes; one of these was doing tight turns round the Cisk Brewery chimney, while two 109s made diving attacks on him; another was trying to climb gamely up to their level, all were having circles made round them. The four Spits got back safely, claiming a 109 and an 88 destroyed and an 88 probable.

Visited Nippy and Australia in the evening in hospital. Nippy rather bruised and shaken, but not much the worse. Said he got on the tail of an 88 and followed it into the barrage; remembers diving after it, firing, then nothing till he found himself falling head-first towards Valetta, wondering where his aeroplane had got to; he must have been blown out through his harness, hood, and everything else. He pulled the rip-cord and the chute opened; his 88 was one of the early ones, because as he floated down he had to watch stick after stick sail past him and explode underneath, while the flak came whistling up past him from below; he actually landed in a crater which he'd seen made a minute before. Australia still in bed, but as cheerful as ever; told us of his argument with Kurt, the German prisoner, on the subject of discipline versus initiative. Kurt admitted that he was shot down because he was following his No. 1, and wasn't watching his own tail. Australia tried to persuade him that if he'd been on his own he would have seen MacQ coming and broken away. No, no, said Kurt, he couldn't have done that; if he had, he would have lost touch with his No 1, and his No 1 would have been alone. Alone with about 48 other 109s, said Australia. Kurt still thinks Germany will win: Russia will be dealt with this summer and then they will turn on us; it may, however, take up to 18 months. He also says that Malta will be invaded and that within a month *he* will be bringing *us* cigarettes instead of vice versa.

Saturday 11.4.42
Mac is found to have pulled a cartilage in his throat and has been grounded. Jimmie of course insists that this is not the result of having to bale out, but of inability to stop talking about it afterwards; in any case he for one can't see what Mac is so proud

about – if he'd been bloody careless and got himself shot down in a 25,000 dollar ship he wouldn't go bragging all over the place about it. Now Mike has gone unserviceable, too, with a sprained ankle; Australia is still in hospital; B … considered too inexperienced to fly here, so we are rather short of pilots, especially section-leaders. Daren't admit it, though, in case we have to give up some of our readiness to 249.

Can't understand the Hun; after Tuesday's raids aimed at Valetta he has reverted to legitimate objectives and apparently abandoned the assault on morale. For once he seems to be hesitating to be ruthless; perhaps he does intend to invade and wants everything to be in working order.

We always seem to be hungry here, it must be the sea-air I think. Don't know what we should do if we couldn't get plenty of eggs; the Maltese keep chickens on their flat roofs, if there is no room on the ground, and at the moment at any rate eggs are plentiful. We usually have two for breakfast and two for tea. Lunch and dinner are always the same, Maconochie or corn-beef; it's quite good, but we're all sick of it already. Bread is getting short, too, and sometimes they give us dog-biscuits instead. That's what they taste like, anyway. The chocolate ration is two small packets a week; I hoard mine like a miser and if possible trade my cigarettes for more.

On some evenings we feel so hungry that we have dinner in the mess and then go out to Carrie Busuttil's pub and have eggs and chips, four fried eggs and sometimes a pork chop for good measure. She cooks the sweetest chips I think I've ever had; we asked her the secret and she said she cooked them in a mixture of olive-oil and lard, the more olive-oil the better.

Still no aircraft, usual raids.

Sunday 12.4.42
Had an early lunch and started out for the aerodrome with Goldie to come to readiness at 1300; midday raid caught us half-way there, so we went to the Bofors again. 88s came over in the usual strength, and one wave attacked the aerodrome and offered the gun some targets. When they had gone, half a dozen 109s came down in line abreast and did some ground-strafing of the aerodromes and dispersals; found this more shaking than I'd imagined. As pilot,

A spitfire in its pen on Malta.

thinking of the vulnerability of aircraft, I'd always 'held that
advantage lay with troops on the ground if they took proper cover
and used their automatic weapons; still think that's true, but would
add that troops seasoned to it would be far more effective than fresh
ones. First experience is somewhat bewildering: the aircraft arrive
almost before their roar, they are difficult to identify quickly in the
head-on position and the rattle of cannon and machine-gun is so
threatening and pervasive that it's hard to tell whether the one which
is pointing at you, or another, is firing. One of the 109s passed right
over the post at about 20 feet, going like a ding-bat, and Goldie had
a shot at him with a rifle; we watched him pull his ha-ha boost and
sail effortlessly up to a couple of thousand feet. Went on to the
aerodrome and found they had hit a Spit on the ground and set the
rudder on fire; another cannon shell had hit the wind-shield, but
done nothing more than star it. Both our aircraft became
unserviceable, so no readiness after all.

Sometimes, when we can put up no aircraft at all, Fighter Control
lays on a dummy R/T Conversation. The other day, after a corporal
in a cubicle had announced that he'd spotted four 109s and was

going to attack them, the German listening service picked it up and broadcast a warning, which confused the Huns so much that there was a good deal of nattering in high-pitched German and finally a burst of cannon-fire.

Tedder, the C-in-C Middle East, has been here; he's said to have been pretty impressed by the scale of the raiding; don't think anyone realises how heavy it is until they see it. As a result of the belief that the great man was going to inspect all billets, sheets mysteriously appeared on our beds, although we'd been told for three weeks that there were none in the island; made us feel somewhat surly.

Sat out on the Bastion in the evening; there's no proper ante-room in the mess, so we often do this, and on a fine night it makes a very good substitute. Talk turned on shooting stars, light-years and the universe, not a subject any of us knew much about. Mac, as usual, had the last words when he observed, rather dogmatically: 'Space ain't a goddam thing,' and then added, half guardedly, half defiantly, 'not if it's real space'. There was nothing more to say.

VI

Monday 13.4.42

Italian radio claimed thirteen Spits destroyed here yesterday; there were none airborne that day. Pete and I went in to Valetta; I took the opportunity to have a look at Queen Victoria in front of the Public Library; the crater is not fifty feet away but the Good Queen has not moved a muscle.

I had been reading a book about the Knights in Malta and was struck by the parallel between the Order as it was then and the Service as it is to-day. There were certain obvious differences, it is true, but they did not affect the fundamental likeness. For instance the Order was recruited only from a certain caste, and proof of nobility for four generations on either side was required of the aspirant; the Service disregards class, creed and colour. The Order was a professional one; the Service, at its fighting level, is more predominantly amateur. The Order was religious; the Service is secular.

One imagines that the last difference was more apparent than real, and that the rank and file of the younger Knights did not differ greatly from the rank and file of pilots. There must have been some, particularly in the early days, who took the devotional side of their lives seriously, but the bulk of them seem to have been as interested in the bright lights as we are. I thought of them as something between subalterns and hearty or wealthy undergraduates.

The book mentioned the constant friction between the older and young generations; one pictured an operational type grumbling about that old dead-beat so-and-so, and another agreeing that he was terrible, still thinking in terms of Lepanto. They must have been a tough race in their best days: the garrison of St Angelo during the great siege fought to the last man without thought of surrender, young and old, Knight and man-at-arms alike.

The hotels the Knights built for themselves in Valetta are roughly contemporary with the colleges of Oxford and Cambridge and, in spite of the difference in architecture, reminiscent of them.

I used to think of the Knights and try to picture their way of life. In some ways, not so much because of their militant rather than humanistic outlook, as because of their organisation into languages, the Order resembled the Service rather than a University. These languages must have corresponded to the national squadrons of the RAF; once it was Castile, Provence, Italy, Auvergne, Aragon; now it is Rhodesia, Poland, Australia, Norway, Czecho-Slovakia, New Zealand, Canada, Belgium, the United States.

This comparison suggested others. Prussia since Frederick the Great and Germany since Bismarck had proved as much an enemy of Christendom as ever the Turk was. Now, as in 1565, Malta was a bastion subjected to a merciless siege.

What interested me particularly was to know how far we resembled and how far we differed from our predecessors. They lived on the eve of the period of nationalism, we live perhaps on its morrow; if we could compare them with ourselves, their Order with our Service, we should know whether we had progressed further from it than they had advanced towards it.

To answer this question it was necessary to determine what it was in the RAF which had enabled it to do what it had done. Why should the League of Nations, with all the idealism in the world behind or in it, have failed and the RAF, which never admits to any ideals at all, have succeeded? The more I thought about it the more astonishing it seemed. Before the war the Service undoubtedly had an indifferent reputation, not only among Magistrates and Insurance Companies, but with a large body of well-meaning people. Its officers were often not considered to be gentlemen and pilots as a whole were thought tough, wild and unmannerly. The horse was still the hallmark by which the officer-class was judged, and manners and a correct address were still more important than imagination or ability. By these standards the RAF was tried and failed.

What was it then which enabled the Service to command the loyalty of squadrons recruited from all the Dominions, half a dozen European countries, and the United States? What was it that enabled all these elements to mix together without favour or friction? They undoubtedly did. It was a Polish squadron which emerged from the Battle of Britain with the best record of any unit of any nationality, yet I had never heard a hint of envy or detractive explanation from British pilots on this score. The CO of this squadron was an Englishman and one of his Flight Commanders a Canadian. During 1941 the most successful squadron was for some months an Australian one, later American; this produced rivalry but no malice. In the Eagle Squadron in which I had been a Flight Commander criticism and appraisement was directed more against the sister squadrons than against the surrounding foreigner. In my first squadron two Czech sergeant pilots had begged to remain with us even when they were offered places in a Czech squadron which was then being formed. I myself had been extremely sorry to leave the Americans. A man's best friend was usually one of his own kind, but the division went no deeper than this; cliques and national antipathies were unknown.

I wondered whether hatred of the enemy could account for this fellowship, but rejected the explanation at once; none of the English-speakers felt any real hatred at all. I wondered whether a sense of common purpose would explain it, but this theory was no more satisfactory than the other; the average pilot is too deeply involved in the war to be able to think in terms of common enemies or common aims. I wondered whether it could be explained as a fellowship of the air and felt that this was nearer the mark.

The air is an element more brutal than the sea and more searching. It is impossible to live by it and have many illusions either about yourself or about those around you; if you do it will expose you or them before long. If there is one quality which pilots possess it is genuineness. I do not know whether this is an element attracted by the air or an attribute imposed by it, but I felt it was the virtue which underlay and explained what had seemed so puzzling.

This theory seemed to fit the facts. What the layman had once regarded as lack of manners was partly uncouthness or lack of consideration, but partly also a refusal to show an interest which was not felt or say a thing which was not believed. In this light the uncouthness of the airman seemed pardonable and the manners of say Brett Young's Essendines hollow and meaningless.

I began to understand why cowardice was merely pitied or disregarded, but line-shooting was actively and cordially disliked. The coward was just a poor devil who had not the nerve, as another might not have the eyesight, to do a job; but a line-shooter was un-genuine and beyond the pale. This was the criterion by which the RAF judged and beside it other things had small importance. Birth and upbringing counted for nothing; nationality and creed did not matter; learning or ignorance, wealth or poverty, skill or ham-handedness in flying, dullness or eccentricity in everyday life, it was the same: if a man was genuine he was a good type, if un-genuine he was not.

It was this criterion of straightforwardness, I thought, which made it possible for all manner of men of all nations to work together as they did. A man was not judged by any of the old standards, race, birth, religion, wealth or membership of the best clubs, but according to his personal integrity; if he passed the test the other things did not matter, if he failed they would not help him. It followed naturally that a Service which applied a universal standard should command a universal loyalty.

I wondered whether the same could have been said of the Order. It might have been true in the early days when it seemed as if the Turk might overrun Europe and the Knights fought for their faith and not their purses, but it was improbable that such a spirit could have lasted into the period of power and prosperity. There were too many factors hostile to it. Birth was still all-important; money had begun to matter; the rigid division of the Order into languages, living in separate hotels and charged with the defence of separate bastions and forts, must have generated internal jealousy and rivalry.

Comparing what I had read of the Order and knew of the Service I felt that we had outstripped them. Except for purely religious bodies, I suppose the Knights were the last of the great international Orders; it did not seem too much to hope that the RAF would be the first of the new ones. International recruitment or control of a Service has always been decried; now the RAF has laid the bogey and shown that it can be worked. It appears that Europe, which was sickening with nationalism in the days of the Knights, is convalescent again. I hope to goodness someone remembers this when peace is being made: to me it seems the most important discovery of the war.

Tuesday 14.4.42
Another morning on the aerodrome building our pen. Work interrupted by a raid: twelve 88s appeared, heading straight for us; they showed no signs of turning off, so down the shelter we went. It was 15-20 feet deep in the rock, but part of it had already collapsed once under a direct hit, and there was only one entrance, so none of us felt particularly confident; even there we could hear the whistle of the bombs and feel the waves of blast. Found myself counting, just like taking a beating at school; emerged to find everything shrouded in dust; don't know how near they fell, but it can't have been very far.

Later watched two 109s shooting up Luqa; they climbed to 3,000 feet, turned and went back again; this time only one of them pulled out, a column of black smoke showed what had happened to the other. Bad tactics. This compensated for the news that Kelly had been shot down; he'd baled out at 800 feet but the chute had failed to open properly and he'd hit the water very hard and had then got caught up in the shroud lines; in disentangling himself he'd lost his dinghy. The two Wests had gone out to patrol him until the rescue launch could pick him up; they found him a couple of miles off-shore swimming quite strongly without his trousers, but making no apparent progress; he even put up two fingers at them and blew through his moustache. Or so they say. Rescued later, little the worse.

MacQ and Bob Sergeant later levelled the score with a 109 between them. Wing-Co said the Hun R/T was diverting: they were complaining of heavy escort over the rescue-launch and calling for reinforcements, when actually three Hurricanes were holding off about a dozen of them. In the evening the AOC called us all together and told us that replacements of aircraft were on their way and would arrive within three weeks at the outside; there's going to be the hell of a tough battle when they arrive. Johnny Plagis's girl friend, Anne Policino, coined a new phrase to-day – called Mac a great shoot-liner.

Wednesday 15.4.42
Cold wind blowing out of Africa has brought thick weather; no aerial activity of any sort. Worked on our blast-pen in the morning and

played bridge all the afternoon; Mac and I, usually too ambitious a combination to be successful, won nine bob.

There are all sorts of rumours flying about: the most common one is that the Hun is leaving Sicily to-day, next week, in the middle of May; it was to have been at Easter, but he didn't go. Another, that he has announced his intention of bombing Musta and M'dina Cathedrals. A third, that he knows where we are quartered and has issued a warning that he intends to wipe out the place; the fact that to do so would be more in his tradition than the present concentration on legitimate objectives adds to its force. The latest Maltese story is that a convoy of three American aircraft-carriers is bringing not less than 150 Spits to the island; that's the silliest one we've yet heard. These rumours play on alarm and despondency on one hand, and unfounded hopes on the other; they're probably the work of Fifth Columnists; there are said to be a certain number of these about and, as in France, it is not a case of the higher the fewer.

Managed to get a shave and a bath. Not easy for me with an electric-razor, because the juice seems to be off two days out of three from bomb damage. Baths are rationed to one a week.

Thursday 16.4.42
Weather still dud. Our papers are bragging about 1,000 tons of bombs dropped on the Ruhr in a week; should say this is just about the same as our weekly ration: we get a hundred or more 88s, each with a ton and three-quarters of bombs, six days out of seven. Admittedly they have advantages, interior lines again, and a very short round trip, but on the other hand they have had the losses of both the Battle of Britain and the eastern front, yet seem almost as strong as ever. There is no doubt they have a bloody good aircraft in the Ju 88; it is fast, well-armed, heavily armoured, very strongly made, carries a heavy load and has a good range. Everyone here has the greatest respect for it, and I've heard several say they think it's the outstanding aircraft of the war.

Beauforts went out to attack a convoy east of here yesterday; out of eight, two were shot down over the target, three near the island on their way back, and one as it landed; from the last one the pilot was killed but the rest of the crew escaped with wounds. They claim three torpedo-hits, but my God, those boys take a beating. Wish we could do more to help. The Beaufighter escort got two 110s to help to level the scores. It looks as if the spring offensive will start soon; my guess is still that he will push a trident through the Caucasus, Asia Minor and North Africa; it looks as if Cyprus is going to be important this year.

Heard that the 109 pilot shot down by Buck Buchanan the other day was Kurt's Staffel-Kapitän, Neuhof by name. He claims 38 victories and only needed two more for his Ritterkreuz; apparently he has fought in France, Battle of Britain, Russia, Libya, and here; 22 of his victories are Russian. He was very eager to meet the pilot who had shot him down, so Buck went to see him in hospital and got him to sign his log-book.

I heard later that Neuhof was vain enough to be disappointed in Buck, who at that time had only one ring and no gong; seemed to think he wasn't distinguished enough to have shot him down. He said that he had pulled up after attacking a Hurricane and had never seen what hit him; he seemed to think that his No. 2 had failed him by not protecting his tail. Buck was flying along not knowing there was anything near him, when a 109 appeared in his sights; all he had to do was to press the button; range and deflection were both right. Neuhof said he was hit by what must have been the first burst and baled out at once, but Buck never saw him get out and continued to attack the empty machine almost all the way down to the ground.

Friday 17.4.42
Weather still bad, so no activity in the air; the lull has lasted three days now. Put in another morning with the sandbags and an idle afternoon. A swastika has appeared in the mess, taken off an 88 which the Beaus shot down the other night; it tried to make a forced landing at Luqa, but missed the runway, hit the wall and burnt out. A brownish smear across the panel is said to be the rear-gunner's blood, don't know if that's true. No mail yet.

Saturday 18.4.42
Still no aircraft, so another morning with the sandbags. Four raids to-day, instead of the usual two or three, but the scale seemed smaller, only about 30 bombers in each instead of 50 to 80.

A party to celebrate gongs for MacQueen and Johnny Plagis.

(*Right*) Buck Buchanan.

(*Below*) Spitfires and Beau-
fighters on Malta.

Whisky, gin and liqueurs still seem plentiful, but there isn't very much serious drinking, just an occasional celebration. Personally I daren't, to fly here with a hangover would be the shortest cut to glory I know.

Sunday 19.4.42
Sandbags again.

VII

Monday 20.4.42

On our way to the aerodrome when we heard aircraft overhead and twelve Spits flew out of the west in formation, followed by another twelve and two bunches of eleven, 46 in all. Always find sight and sound of a large formation is affecting, but this was so welcome and unexpected that it made us all absurdly excited. We couldn't think where they'd all come from; general opinion was that it must have been from the Middle East, because they were too many to have come off the *Eagle* or even the *Eagle* and *Argus* together. It was lucky they arrived half an hour after the morning raid, we were able to get them stowed away in their pens before another could develop.

We asked which and how many carriers had brought them out, and were amazed to learn that it was all done by one, the USS *Wasp*, which had fetched them all the way from England. It was one of the most secret things there had ever been; they had known nothing themselves until they had gone on board; it was certainly news to us, yet Maltese rumour, though it was exaggerated and distorted, had got hold days ago of the essential fact of the nationality of the carrier. It beats me. The two new squadrons are 601 and 603; this time they have brought them out as squadrons, not assembled a number of pilots who have never seen each other before and given them a designation. Provided that they have plenty of experienced people it should work better.

Missed lunch and drove over to Luqa to come to readiness on the new aircraft. Found they had been dispersed all over the place and no one seemed to know which were serviceable and which weren't. The armourers had left a job unfinished on mine, and I spent hours trying to find them, but without success; finally a sergeant turned up in a bus and said he could find me another one which was definitely serviceable, and I followed him over to it.

Malaya brought round some most welcome tea, only a couple of sandwiches, but very acceptable. Talked to the crew on my new machine and discovered they belonged to a Blenheim squadron and that this was their first experience of Spits, they hadn't even graduated on Hurricanes, and only seemed to have the haziest idea of what they must do. That's a hell of a send-off for us. The aircraft was a Spit VC with an armament of four cannon; the mounting seemed to be very neat and it was good to know that the fire power was twice as great as that of the old VB. Some time since I'd last flown and I found myself getting jittery as zero hour approached; what was worse, discovered that I'd left Jumbo, my little white elephant behind; this would be the first time I'd flown without him since B. gave him to me last August. Always wore him round my neck, but I'd put him in my pocket in the morning when taking off my shirt, and then changed my trousers.

At 1720 we heard the sirens sounding all over the island; wondered why we hadn't already been scrambled, we usually took off long before the alert. Climbed into my machine, strapped myself in and put on my helmet and gloves; at last the Very light, which was the signal to scramble, was shot off. Learnt afterwards that the delay was caused by the telephone lines being down; this prevented us from gaining enough altitude before the bombers came in. There were to have been six of us, but Chris failed to get away; the other five took off and formed up, with Bart leading, Ricky with Jimmie and Tex with me. Dislike a formation of five in line abreast, it's so unwieldy. Noticed that Jimmie and Ricky were lagging behind a little; called them up only to find that the R/T was unserviceable. Worse followed: the wind-shield began to oil up; this often happens with new machines, but I never realised before how much difference it made.

The sky was half overcast with a canopy of high white cloud coming in from the west, thank goodness to have a rest from the usual dazzling sun. We saw six Spits take off from Takali and four Hurricanes from Halfar; with us that made fifteen, the most I'd ever known. We climbed up to 8,000 feet over the island, when Bart seemed to see something; without R/T I didn't know what was going on; we dived towards the north-west and I could see bomb-smoke and dust on Takali, not very much, what you'd expect from a few fighter-bombers. We came down to 3,500 feet without seeing anything hostile, so reformed and began to climb again; over St Paul's Bay, at a higher level than ourselves, we could see a heavy dog-fight in progress.

Climbed in a wide left-hand sweep and came back over Takali at 6,000 feet. I was on the inside of the turn when I suddenly noticed an 88 dive past within 400 yards at 11 o'clock, flying in the opposite direction. I made after him at once and saw him pull out of his dive 1,000 feet below me; he was going bloody fast, so I determined to attack from below, that would give me a chance to gain speed myself in diving after him. At first he seemed to be running away from me; no time to look at my clock, but I must have been making well over 300. Kept a good look-out for 109s, a stern chase like this gives them just the opportunity they want, especially if you get too absorbed in the 88s; saw none, but a stick of bombs released somewhere higher up sailed in a leisurely way past my starboard wing. Thinking of it afterwards I decided it was rather an unusual event, but at the time I made a mental note of it and nothing more; it neither surprised nor alarmed nor interested me. I suppose the only two things which could have done so were 109s and 88s.

I had the throttle through the gate, and gradually the range began to close; as we crossed the coast I decided it had done so and tried to line him up in my sights. I'd been watching him all this time through the side-panels, and hadn't realised how opaque the front panel had become; found that I couldn't see either the 88 or the ring or bead of the reflector sight; fired a short burst in his direction and then decided it was useless and pulled away. Later wished I'd persevered, with all that ammunition and four cannons I might have done him some injury. As I hauled off I noticed a large splash in the sea not far from the coast, a machine had evidently gone in there; there was also something burning on Takali.

Flew back south and an aircraft going in the other direction fired a quick, wild burst at me as we passed, but showed no signs of staying to fight. I pulled the nose up so as to lose some of my speed and give myself a chance of pushing a hand out into the slip-stream to clean the wind-shield, but some 109s arrived – four of them I think – and I began to mill round with them. I'd never flown a VC before, and found it a little heavy; tried to out-turn one of them, but gave it up because I was afraid if I continued to go round in uniform circles one of his friends would begin to practise his deflection shooting without my being able to see him; only saw one of them fire.

Couldn't remember afterwards how I threw them off, but managed to do so, and made after some 88s which had appeared flying south-west after dropping their bombs on Grand Harbour. Again felt the lack of an advantage on height or speed; they were coming out at my level, but were travelling very fast after their long dives from 15,000 feet, whereas I'd been dog-fighting and had lost all my speed in tight turns. Began another stern chase. The nearest one was about 350 yards ahead when I saw a Bofors shell fired at him come up alongside me; he was already out of range, because it burst just as it reached my level, about 50 yards, as near as I could judge from my starboard wing. I even heard the bang.

Crossed the south coast and still wasn't in range; didn't want to jink because this meant a further sacrifice in distance, but thought it would be wiser to do so, as I'd been flying straight and level too long and didn't trust the rear-vision mirror. Just as well I did so, as at that moment two 109s which I hadn't seen anywhere came whistling down from the west and overshot; I think they had been trying to slip in behind me and had been put off by my change of direction. Had begun to strike out again for the 88s, which were further ahead than ever, when I heard the sound of a 109's cannon firing; took most violent evasive action and looked everywhere, but couldn't see a thing. This was new to me and rather shaking; except for the Bofors shell a minute before, this was the first extraneous sound I'd ever heard in an aircraft. No leisure to puzzle it out at the time, but thought about it afterwards and came to the conclusion it must have been the self-destroying ammunition which the Huns sometimes use, bursting very close; curious that I'd neither seen the 109 nor the puffs from the shells.

By this time the 88s had all disappeared. Flew towards Rabat, where another dog-fight seemed to be in progress; spotted two aircraft flying towards me in what looked like 109 formation. Kicked on rudder to get a clearer view through the side-panel; was just in time – as the leader opened fire I pulled up hard in a right-hand climbing turn and both passed underneath. These 109s seem to set

great store by head-on attacks, I wonder how many times they fire
on one another; feel certain they must, they open at such long
range. Convinced myself at last that I was doing no good, so dived
down to the deck and made my way back to Luqa. A great pall of
bomb-dust was just blowing off the western end of the aerodrome;
didn't know whether the runway was serviceable after the raid, so
flew low round the perimeter trying to make certain there were no
new craters on it and hoping someone would give me a green light
from the ground. Third time round, as I was approaching the
smoke-pall, I saw two 109s dive through it across my bows not more
than 300 yards ahead. They were obviously going to shoot up the
aerodrome and I felt sure they hadn't spotted me, so I turned hard
left and went through the cloud after them. Re-emerged over the
field at 50 feet and knew they must be a short distance ahead, but
couldn't see them anywhere; was in the act of cursing my oily
wind-shield, when suddenly, without warning, there was a vivid
flash and I felt rather than heard a tremendous bang. The stick,
which had felt taut and sensitive in my hand, seemed to sag and
become quite limp; knew at once that the aircraft had been vitally
hit and was out of control, knew too that this must be the end – it
might fly on another couple of hundred yards, but then it would
keel over one way or the other and take me into the ground with it.

I remember feeling surprised and thinking rather bitterly that my
belief that I should survive had been a myth after all. At that time I
had no hope whatever, it was as if I'd been in a racing car doing
about 100 when the steering-gear had failed; I was so close to the
ground that it felt rather like that; the only difference was that I was
50 feet up and doing 200. But instead of going down, the aircraft
began to climb very steeply, and as the nose went up so the port
wing went down, as if we had begun to do a climbing roll to the left.
I jammed the stick into the forward right-hand corner of the
cockpit, and this seemed to prevent the machine from making its
climb a vertical one, or executing rolls in the course of it, but we
were still both tilted and banked at about 60°; however, there was
hope. I had to hold the stick forward with my right hand, and with
my left I began to undo my harness and extracted the pin
successfully. I'd decided that I couldn't risk being held to the
machine by the R/T cable and oxygen-tube as I tried to jump; I

should have little speed and there wouldn't be enough centrifugal force to snap them, so they might tie me to the aircraft and take me down with it. Therefore I had to get rid of my helmet before I began to get out. All I had to do was to loosen one chin-strap and it would come off easily. I fumbled for this strap with my left hand, but I was wearing thick Canadian gloves and had no sense of touch, also I suppose I was preoccupied with keeping the machine under some sort of control; I couldn't find it and began to grow desperate.

By this time most of the speed had fallen away, but the nose was still elevated at an absurd angle; I felt a stall and a spin would come any time now and knew I should never escape unless I first got rid of that bloody helmet. I gave way momentarily to panic, wrenched the oxygen mask aside and tore wildly at the helmet itself, but with the chin-strap still tight it would not move; then I took hold of myself and undid the strap methodically. If the machine had stalled at the top of its climb and spun I should have been too late, because I didn't get rid of the helmet until this danger had already passed; don't know whether I had subconsciously kicked on bottom rudder, or whether it was normal nose-drop, but the spinner had fallen to the horizon and we were in level though precarious flight. Nothing would correct the 60° bank to port, and I noticed it had already turned us round to face the other way; when first hit I'd been in the middle of the aerodrome flying east and was now just off the northern perimeter flying west. Looked at the altimeter and saw 900 feet; that was enough, so pushed the stick hard forward and felt myself rise from the seat and shoot half out of the cockpit; then I was stranded.

I was sitting on the starboard wall of the cockpit with my head and shoulders in the open and my legs inside; the chute had caught somewhere and was holding me fast; the aircraft had fallen off in a left-hand spiral dive and the ground looked incredibly close. I tried to shake myself free, but the machine had gathered speed and the slipstream as well as the chute was pinning me down. I tried to lever myself over the obstruction with my arms, but the strength of the wind made me feel puny and helpless. I knew it was hopeless to get back into the cockpit and try to regain control. It was now or never; 1,000 feet is usually given as the minimum safe height for jumping, I'd never have had more than 900 and now half of that must have been lost. I felt trapped and desperate and as a last resort I threw my head and shoulders back as hard as I could in a backward somersault. Free at last.

I was turning over and over so fast that the movement seemed to confuse my arms, and when my hand reached for the rip-cord it wasn't where it should have been; I had to make three separate grabs before I found it. As the chute opened the sensation was as if a giant was swinging me round his head by the scruff of the neck, then suddenly the world, which had been whirling round, came right side up. I looked up and made sure that the canopy had opened properly and then wondered whether 109s would shoot me up before I reached the ground, but immediately realised how silly that was, I was only 150 feet up and seemed to be falling astonishingly fast; just had time to see my machine hit the deck a couple of hundred yards away on the other side of a small ravine when I was bracing myself for my own landing. I wasn't swinging at all and dropped straight on to a rocky terrace and immediately fell forward on my hands and knees; luckily the chute collapsed at once, so I just lay where I was, panting and sweating as if I'd run a quarter, but profoundly thankful to be alive. I could see the aeroplane blazing furiously and could hear the ammunition exploding in the heat; that was the only sight and sound; the bomb dust seemed to have drifted away, and everything else was calm and normal. One of the first thoughts that occurred to me was that this was what came of leaving my little elephant behind.

After a few minutes voices approached and I thought I'd better stand up and declare myself; a group of Tommies appeared, and I shouted 'British' and then felt rather foolish, because they never seemed to have been in any doubt of the fact. They took me to the mess of ack-ack headquarters, where I was given a drink and a wash and allowed to telephone. I was surprised and rather pleased to find how unmoved I was by what had happened; pouring myself out a beer I noticed my hand was quite steady, only hoped there wouldn't be a reaction later. No one turned up to take me home, so I stayed with the soldiers and had quite a party; one of these later drove me back to the mess in the Colonel's car.

The electricity had failed and the mess was lit by candles. I went upstairs with my chute over my arm and got quite a welcome from some of the 249 boys; we went to the bar for a final drink and I tried to find out what had happened to the others. They had been operating from Luqa and had apparently not returned; all the telephones were down and there was no news of them. This seemed strange, because it was already late.

I went up to see John Lodge, the Intelligence Officer, but he told the same story. At this moment Bart turned up; he said he was the only one of our five who had landed back at Luqa and he didn't know where the other three were, all the telephones had failed and he hadn't been able to find out anything. We rang Fighter Control, but they couldn't tell us any news of them, though they thought that one had landed safely at Takali. I walked round to the billets to see if there was any sign of Jimmie and found him in bed; thank goodness, that was one more; he was the one who had landed at Takali. It looked as if the other two were missing. There was nothing more to be done, so went to bed.

Tuesday 21.4.42

Slept well and had no bad dreams; I'd bruised my heel landing and it was painful when I put my weight on it, but there was no other damage except abrasions on both knees and one elbow.

Heard that Tex had flown into a wireless mast yesterday; at first it was thought that this was an accident, but when his body was recovered it was found that he had been killed by cannon-fire. This was bad news for me, I'd known him well and helped to train him; glad to think he got his 88 first. No news at all of Ricky; he was a little too intrepid for these conditions and probably followed an 88 too far and got jumped by the waiting 109s; the splash I'd seen in the sea might have been from his aircraft. Wonder how poor young Chris is going to take it, they trained together and were inseparable. Talked to Bart and Jimmie and found they had failures too; Jimmie R/T and wind-shield, like me and Bart R/T and cannon; suppose these are unavoidable when you have to fly new and untried machines.

Three heavy raids, principally directed at Luqa and Takali, the Hun is clearly aiming at our new aircraft. Their bombing is good, but they seem to be lucky in the matter of direct hits. With their bigger bombs near misses are as good as hits, because the blast blows the wall of the pen on to the aircraft, but at any distance, or against the smaller bombs, the pens have proved effective. Difficulty is one side has to be left open for entry and exit; all this month the Army and workmen have been trying to lessen this gap by extending one or other of the side walls in a screening curve, but the field of vulnerability can only be narrowed, not excluded altogether. Quite apart from what is being lost by direct bomb damage – blast, splinter, and fire – there is a steady indirect drain on serviceability by damage caused by falling ack-ack shrapnel. Killeen says that when the Takali barrage has been in action an average of two aircraft are hit in this way; he complains bitterly that it is always those that are nearly serviceable. One of the pens hit to-day was the one we'd been building – not a very big bomb, but it tore the Spit to shreds, burnt it out, and demolished a month's work for good measure. Pete Nash was on the aerodrome, noticed the fire and ran out to see if he could do anything; he was caught in the open by the next wave of bombers, looked up and saw diving 88s right overhead, remembers hearing a short, intense whistle and all the air being sucked out of his lungs, then nothing more till he came to on the ground fifteen yards away and, he thinks, about fifteen minutes later. On the whole he was lucky to have been spared seeing the rest of the raid by being unconscious; still pretty shaken.

We watched the afternoon raid from the roof of the mess: this time Kesselring craftily sent over a dummy raid at 4.30 p.m. and all the Spits took off; the real raid didn't materialise until 5.20, and at 6 o'clock when the Spits were trying to land a fresh wave of 109s came in to do some circuit-strafing. It was agonising to watch the tired Spits, with no ammunition and seriously short of fuel, circling the field and trying to pick a path to land among the new craters under continual harassment. Time and again it looked as if one must be lost; the 109s would come diving out of the sun in the west – always in pairs – and at the last moment the Spit – when everyone had been wondering whether he'd seen them or not, and had just come to the conclusion that he couldn't have, and given him up for lost – would turn in to the 109s and they would flash past, firing furiously; then followed the terrible suspense to see whether the Spit had been hit, finally relief to see it still flying. The Hun No 2s contributed very little, they seemed to be there to guard their leader's tail and

Building stone blast pens on Malta.

Spitfire V which suffered bomb-damage.

confirm his victories in the Richthofen tradition. Once a No 2 was perfectly placed behind a Spit, almost stalled in a climbing turn, but he failed to take the opportunity. Later two jumped MacQueen when he was on the point of touching down; he said afterwards that his fuel gauge showed zero and he saw them coming but didn't dare go round again; he was an absolutely sitting shot, but the leading 109 must have been windy of the ground-defence, he fired a long burst, but missed, and his No 2 didn't fire. The two Bofors and the machine-guns did their best, and probably saved MacQueen, but there weren't nearly enough of them and the lack of 20-mm. cannon was felt. Some of the boys were badly shot up, but all got down safely. Bob Sergeant was attacked by six 109s, felt himself hit, spun, corrected, spun the other way and the motor cut out. He came out at 200 feet and coaxed the motor in again; controls were so heavy he thought the rudder and elevator trim must have been shot away; looked behind and found one elevator hanging like a broken shutter; he couldn't climb or raise more than 140 mph, but wasn't molested again and brought the machine safely home.

Chris helped to solve the question of what hit me yesterday: he told me he saw two 109s fly across Luqa ground-strafing, he took a shot at them with his revolver and was then knocked down by the blast of a bomb dropped by an 88 which he hadn't noticed. The flash I'd seen was much too large to be that of a cannon-shell; I'd had the impression of a bomb-burst, but hadn't been certain whether it was a bomb some distance away or a Bofors shell in the aircraft. The two 109s which Chris saw must have been the same two that I'd chased and the bomb which bowled him over must have thrown me out of control. Probably the blast had knocked the port control surfaces upward out of alignment: that would account for the behaviour of the machine afterwards. Hell of a way to be shot down, but by and large feel glad it wasn't 109s; this was hardly my fault.

Terribly sorry for Chris; he only looks about sixteen and he thought the world of Ricky.

Goldie opened his score to-day with a 109, one of four which attacked him and Jimmie, and the CO entered double figures with a brace of 88s. Apparently he became separated from the others, so he flew to Filfla (a rock four miles south of the island) and circled there at 5,000 feet hoping the bombers would come out his way. His R/T would receive, but not transmit; he heard someone call up and say: 'Look out, Wombat aircraft, there's something over Filfla', and later the voice of one of his own sergeant-pilots came through with: 'Keep your eyes open, Wombat, that little bastard's still mucking about over Filfla'; this put him in such a good mood that when the 88s came out he got two of them in quick succession and watched them go down close to each other in the sea. The 109s didn't so much as come near him. His guardian-angel must be a 4-cannon job; think he knows it too; he has twice been shot up here, his neck after his accident – it was slightly broken in the Battle of Britain – only allows his head to turn one way, and he's short-sighted, but he remains cheerfully intrepid and his attitude to the Hun is expressed in his invariable: '109s? Of course I never see 'em!' He reckons this is tougher, if anything, than the Battle of Britain.

Two pilots who arrived with the last batch of Spits have been posted to us, both Americans, Florida and Tiger. Afraid Booker is missing; this was his first flight here, but he had a lot of experience at home; no one saw anything of him after they split up to attack the 88s.

To-day, for the first time, I noticed the inscription on the sun-dial in the roof garden:

Tell ye hours
Amid ye flowers

So pleasantly inappropriate to our present situation as to be worth recording.

VIII

Wednesday 22.4.42

A day with three more heavy raids, again directed at the two fighter-aerodromes. Some nice little verses entitled 'Kesselring's Easter Hymn' have appeared; as near as I can remember, they run:

'Tis Holy Thursday, let us snooker
All the bloody Spits at Luqa,
Forward Messerschmitt and Stuka –

Hallelujah!

Good Friday, it is Halfar's turn,
Prang the crews, the aircraft burn,
Will the blighters ever learn?

Hallelujah!

Now Kampfgeschwaders, rise and shine,
Mix Takali's medicine
'Satan' works like No 9.

Hallelujah!

The Lord is risen, so ply the whip,
Smite the island, thigh and hip,
Tear if off a Safi strip,

Hallelujah!

('Satan' is the name the Huns give one of their heaviest bombs; No 9 is an old-fashioned British medicine.)

Watched all the raids from the roof of the mess. They nearly always attack Takali from the north-east or the south-west; sometimes the aircraft appear to be diving straight at you and the bombs are either released when they are overhead or, if they let them go high, when they are still approaching; you can hear the whistle much more clearly, too. The experts say that it is safer to be on the near side of the target than the far, because bombs more often over- than under-shoot. Certainly it was a bomb which over-shot that did the damage to the old mess. Most of the 88s to-day carried four 500-pounders and eight 250s; the bombing was again good.

You don't often see anything spectacular, in spite of the intensity of the barrages and the combats. Watching a dog-fight from the ground you would think it the most leisurely affair, and it's almost impossible to imagine that the pilots are not circling warily round each other, but are in fact yanking their aircraft round until the g pulls their eyeballs down on to their Adam's-apples.

Other day saw a Stuka, hit in the barrage, fall into Valetta in two pieces. On another occasion an 88 must have received a direct hit from the heavy ack-ack; it broke into such small pieces that we could only see two of them, and the larger was so small it hardly fell faster than one of the crew in a parachute. Once a Ju 88, which had seemed to be flying steadily back to Sicily, suddenly developed a red head to its black body. It continued to fly steadily northward, but we watched the fire grow and increase its possession until, after what seemed like five minutes, from the time it had first caught fire, it ditched in the sea about five miles off-shore. It's comforting to know that the German radio has to inform its listeners, who are beginning to wonder how Malta survives at all, that the island is solid rock and capable of taking a lot of punishment.

Five Wimpies raided Sicily yesterday to counter-bomb his aerodromes; it's something, I suppose, but it's not going to make the hell of a difference.

Bart got two Stukas and Old Bailey an 88, all probable; there was too much opposition for either to confirm them as destroyed. Frank Jemmet crash-landed after being badly shot up by 109s and died in hospital. We'd seen two 109s make a beam-attack on a lone Spit flying just below the brow of the hill behind Verdala Castle; they had each fired a longish burst and we could make out the puffs of their self-destroying ammunition, but the Spit hadn't appeared to be hit and we'd thought no more about it. But Geoff West had happened to be there, he said Jemmet had put it down very prettily on its belly but it had slithered on into a stone wall and the engine had caught fire. Tommies got there almost at once and tried to drag him out, but they hadn't understood the harness and made no headway until Geoff arrived and pulled the pin out for them. If a wall between him and the aircraft hadn't delayed him Geoff thinks they might have saved him, but the Doc says it was the wounds, not the burns, which were fatal. He was a charming boy and very young; I'd had a premonition, but it was probably more rational, because it was his first flight here, than intuitive. A girl in the house where Jemmet was billeted also had a premonition; apparently at the moment when he had come into the room this morning, very pleased because he was to fly for the first time here, a bead had come off the rosary in her hand.

This loss set me thinking about the nature of courage. The local paper the other day referred to the 'stupendous gallantry' of the fighter-pilots and the 'dogged courage' of the gunners. This was flattering, but seemed to me erroneous. For one thing, by its choice of phrase, it seemed to put us at a slightly higher assessment than the gunners, yet my experience with Mike in Valetta had convinced me that the ordeals which we and they were called upon to face were of a different order, and could in no sense be compared.

The man on the ground has nothing to carry him away or take him out of himself. He may or may not have some task to occupy his attention during the period of danger, but at best it can only be something on which, by an imposed or internal discipline, he must force himself to concentrate. He will seldom, as the pilot will, find himself so absorbed and exalted that he is oblivious to all else; danger, fear, even pain. Lying on my face in the dust of that abandoned gun-site, listening to the whistle of bombs I could not see, I had decided that it was the people who fought the night blitzes who were the real heroes of the war. To know that the surrounding fires were the targets for all oncoming bombers, to hear them running up to bomb, to catch the first whistle of the descending bombs, yet to remain doing whatever they had to do, must have called for extraordinary devotion and self-discipline. The pilot's problem is entirely different. In the air everything will happen too quickly, and with too much physical movement and exertion, for fear to take any firm hold. When in imminent danger he will be working at such pressure that he will probably only remember half of the impressions and thoughts which followed each other across his brain, and will have little leisure to be appalled by them. It is not in the air, but on the ground, that he needs courage, for it is there that he will have his worst moments.

I had always been attracted by air-fighting because of the opportunities it gave for initiative and individuality, but I was beginning to find that this had its disadvantages too. These encounters were proving highly personal, and the strain of them was a thing it was impossible to share with anyone else; you fought alone and you had to make your spiritual preparation and hold your mental inquests alone also. I was not dreaming, fortunately, but I found I would usually go to sleep late or wake up early, and lie in bed, turning over and over and over in my mind what had gone before and what was likely to follow after. I had tried to get away from the subject and give my mind to other things, but there was nothing else which would hold my attention – books, local history, sight-seeing all seemed petty and unimportant – and it would always stray back to this over-mastering obsession.

The phrase that had been applied to us – stupendous gallantry – was too close to the popular conception of the fighter-pilot to be accurate. You pictured reckless, carefree, quixotic young men, impervious to physical strain and devoid of complexes. Some pilots might be like that at the beginning of their careers, or they might like to think they were, but this phase seldom lasts long; those with any experience are more often wary, worn, jumpy and disillusioned.

I suppose it is only then that they begin to be brave. Isolated and unpremeditated acts, however daring, are not the ones which deserve recognition. Until there has been some wound, shock, or narrow escape, the instinct of self-preservation is dormant and is easy to control; it is then that acts of daring or recklessness can be done thoughtlessly and without effort. Later, when nerves are ragged and every instinct seeking safety, some inconspicuous task may demand a huge price in self-control. That is courage in its highest form: not so much putting your head into the noose the first five times, when nothing happens, but putting it back a seventh time after the sixth has proved almost fatal. I suppose the quality of courage varies with the effort in self-discipline required to meet a situation; this effort in turn will vary in the first place with the sensibility and imagination of the subject and, in the second, with the extent to which the body's aversion to danger has been exacerbated by his experiences.

I was thankful to have little sensibility. My experience on Monday had given me a new insight into these things and I realised that the really brave man is not the one who takes imperfectly understood chances, but the one who goes on accepting familiar risks with a full knowledge of what they entail. I knew it was still too early to judge whether I had escaped a reaction from having to bale out, but I was feeling well, except for my heel, which was still very painful, and hoped that I had. I wished, though, that there was some visible end to it all.

Thursday 23.4.42
Came to readiness in the afternoon and was to have been first off with Malaya, but went down to the parachute section at what I'd thought was a safe time and lost my scramble to the CO. The two Spits, with two Hurricanes from Halfar, went off against a raid of about 80; we watched the Spits come in, very fast and with beautiful timing, and fall on the Stukas; I don't think a 109 got near them and they came back claiming two probables. I got my kit – all borrowed from Old Bailey after the loss of my own – ready for the next raid, but when it came we weren't sent off; it received a direct hit and of course was all lost. All we could find afterwards was a length of R/T cable; helmet, oxygen-tube, gloves and Mae West had vanished. I've now lost my kit, Old Bailey's kit and the CO's chute.

Luqa, like Takali, is littered with DAs, but no one pays much attention; saw a new 500-pounder to-day, lying flat on the runway, half submerged in the tarmac; there is another behind the dispersal-hut marked, with homely wit, 'u/s return to stores.'

I spoke to an Army corporal about Monday; he told me there was definitely no 109 behind me when I was hit and no Bofors guns were firing, but a stick of bombs had burst on the aerodrome as I'd flown across it. A sergeant said he'd never seen anyone get out of an aeroplane so fast – that's what he thinks – and confirms that the chute opened at about 200 feet. Had my first dream about it last night; rather a comic one in retrospect, though it seemed serious enough at the time. I was coming down by parachute, yet was having a tremendous struggle to lower my undercarriage; swinging in the harness I could find no purchase and the lever had no fulcrum. Thank goodness it was nothing worse than that. Remember after my encounter with a 110 I kept starting out of my sleep thinking that the silence meant that my engine had been hit and had stopped.

Friday 24.4.42
Came to readiness at dawn and at 0730 Chris, Dusty, Shorty and I were scrambled. I led them past Filfla before we even began to climb, then took them up to 15,000 feet about 20 miles south of the island; it was most successful, we never saw a thing. When Woodie told us the bombers were coming in we flew north in a slight dive at 360 IAS; just missed the first raid but ran head-on into the next wave diving on Grand Harbour. I gave the order 'Okay, boys, good luck, good luck', which we had agreed beforehand was to be the signal for a general chase, with every man for himself, and made after the nearest of the 88s.

Before I could get within range four 109s, which I'd seen approaching from the west, came in to attack and I had to leave my bomber and turn to meet them. I had been the most westerly of our four, and hoped to be able to hold the 109s in play long enough to give the others a chance with the 88s; fought a brief engagement with them and saw two of them fire at me, but never got a good opening, so saved my ammunition; we seemed to break off by mutual consent. I flew over Grand Harbour to see if I could find any straggling bandit; they had all disappeared, but the usual patrols of 109s were watching the exits, and I decided to fly out after them. Found them at the same height as myself, and chose one pair which seemed not to have seen me, and tried to stalk them.

Every time I began to get near them I would have to weave to keep my eye on another; once I was almost within range, took a last look round behind me, only to discover that a 109 had nearly crept up on me. I turned left at once and by the time he was within range it was a full deflection shot; he opened fire and I saw those evil smoke tentacles shoot out towards me, but he didn't hit me.

I always watch for them to open fire, but as soon as they have done so I shut my eyes or look elsewhere. Some people watch the tracer with a detached interest; I think I used to, but now I take my evasive action on a snap decision at the outset and hope for the best. Another came in on a beam shot from above; I saw him open fire, took them on the beam or head on. I decided it was useless to go on, because obviously they had all seen me now, so broke away and flew back to Grand Harbour; they didn't follow, probably thinking in their crafty Teutonic minds that I was laying a trap for them.

Was feeling pretty livid at not having fired my guns, when told there was another raid coming in; I ordered the others to re-form and we climbed flat-out back to 8,000 feet. There were 109s above us all the time, but they didn't interfere. Suddenly an 88 with its nose down and its tail right up in the air went past within 100 yards of me. I knew the wave was on its way, because of the flak, but he seemed to have appeared from nowhere; I dived after him flat-out, cut the corner as he pulled out and caught him half-way between Luqa, where he had dropped his bombs, and Valetta.

I waited until I'd closed to 200 yards and then opened fire with a longish burst from dead astern, five-six seconds. I could see the high-explosive incendiary shells exploding as they hit him and what looked like a mixture of black-and-white smoke began to pour from both motors; he turned right-handed very sharply until he was almost standing on his starboard wing-tip. For a moment I hoped he was going to roll over on to his back and dive into the ground; in any case I felt certain he was finished, so pulled away and began to look for another. The other 88s had come out of their dives higher than mine, and I couldn't get up to their height before they reached safety, so turned back and landed without further incident. Found that all the others had got down safely; this was a relief, because Shorty and Dusty haven't been in action here yet; Chris claimed a probable from the first wave and Shorty a damaged. Examined my machine and was glad to find that the 109 hadn't hit me; I always used to feel uncomfortable using the g-pedals, but now put my feet up on them whenever I go into action, they give you much coarser use of rudder and this seems to be a most effective evasive action.

The experience of last month, when Mike and I had tried to climb south of the island and ran our heads into a mass of 109s, made me think that the old hands were right when they said this plan wouldn't work. Since then we'd tried to gain height over or near the island and had still run into trouble, so we'd talked it all over again and decided to give the original plan another trial. We'd asked Fighter Control to scramble us in good time (they could see the plot building up over Sicily long before it reached the island and therefore had plenty of warning) and had determined to gain height as much as 20 miles south of the island. To-day this plan worked splendidly and we'd reached 15,000 feet without any molestation. The lesson of last month was a false one; feel convinced now that the important points are (1) to climb to 15-20,000 feet without being attacked or shadowed (2) to arrive over the target at the same time as the bandits (3) to conserve plenty of height or speed so that the attack on the bombers can be delivered and completed before they reach the protective cordon. The only mistake to-day was in losing too much height in looking for the first wave, otherwise it was encouraging. Bart led the next four in the same way, and he and Chris returned claiming severely damaged 87 and 88; as they came in to land six or eight 109s made a very determined attack on them.

I watched from the mouth of G shelter and once had to dive for safety when I found myself directly in the line of fire of a 109 squirting at a Spit; they all came out unscathed. Never got any confirmation of my 88; felt sick as hell for not having polished him off and thought perhaps I might have exaggerated the damage. But Shorty was underneath it as I attacked and confirmed white smoke from both engines; that would be his glycol streaming out – he could hardly get home without it, but you can't feel much satisfaction without absolute certainty.

Saturday 25.4.42
Came to readiness at Luqa at 1 o'clock and found only two aircraft; Jimmie and Goldie stood by. At 2.30 they were scrambled with orders to join two Spits from Takali and four Hurricanes from Halfar; stood watching them and noticed something fall away from one of them; thought it was a gun-panel but heard later it was the hood. It fell slowly to earth and I guessed that the aircraft would have to land, so quickly put my kit into 'P', which had just become serviceable, and took off as Goldie came in. Hoped to be in time to

Spitfires of 229 Squadron, October 1942.

Servicing a Spitfire in its pen.

find Jimmie; a small voice kept saying that disorganised beginnings are always disastrous, and that to take anyone else's place at the last moment was fatal anyway, but I tried to ignore it and concentrate on catching the others. Called Woodie and was told they hadn't waited, but vector 230° would take me to them. Flew past Filfla and began to climb fast, thinking I should be sure to see them sooner or later; reached 18,500 feet without doing so, transmitted for fix and asked for a fresh vector. Woodie told me they were east of me, so flew that way and climbed 21,000 feet, but still saw nothing.

Sky and sea were both a brilliant blue, but the horizon was hazy, and Malta, 20 miles to the north, was half-hidden in it. I might have been alone in the Mediterranean, and began to feel very lonely. Called for another fix and flew north as instructed, still no sign of the others. I could see the island plainly now, which somehow was comforting, but decided the risk of being picked up by a patrol of 109s was greater there, so reluctantly retreated southward again, out of sight.

Felt more lonely than ever and very tail-conscious; I'd always flown with my hood open even before I had to bale out and can never face anything else now, but it let the cold in and cold always made me feel frightened. The sun was so treacherously bright that whenever my back was towards it I'd whip round half expecting to see something coming out of it, and every time the R/T crackled I'd give a guilty start. Thank goodness it was still working, though, I at least knew what was going on. Flew round in figures of eight, turning towards the sun each time, and trying to search the sky methodically for other aircraft; by this time I'd given up hope of finding the others, but was determined not to be jumped myself.

How much longer were those bloody bombers going to be? At last I heard Woodie say we were to come in now; listened anxiously to hear the others acknowledge, but there was no reply; didn't know what to do. If I went in and they hadn't heard it, I should arrive alone, but if I didn't go in and they had heard it, I should still arrive alone, and that was the last thing I wanted. I called Woodie and asked whether Wombat Leader had received the last message; Woodie said he did not know but would repeat it; this time Red 3 acknowledged it and passed it on to Red Leader. I knew they would be flying towards the island now, so did the same. Afterwards I discovered that Jimmie's R/T had failed at the crucial moment and he hadn't heard the message, but the Hurricanes had apparently done so and acted on it without acknowledgement; the result was they arrived three to four minutes before me and, as it happened, made a perfect interception and destroyed two 88s without any interference from 109s.

I arrived over Grand Harbour at 15,000 feet and there were no bombers to be seen, though smoke and dust below showed that one wave had already passed. I saw two 109s pass a long way below me, and next moment the R/T said 'Look out, lone Spitfire over Grand Harbour, two 109s below you, two 109s below you'; someone on the ground had been pretty spry. I orbited and kept a very sharp look-out. Presently six 109s in pairs swept round from the south-west below me; two of them were directly underneath and I could have jumped them beautifully, but decided to keep my ammunition for the 88s. Later a couple – possibly the same ones – pulled up and attacked, both fired wide and flew away north; decided they would probably shadow me and try again when they thought I wasn't looking. Felt the peculiar agitation and petulance that comes when you think you are going to miss a train: wouldn't those bloody bombers ever come? Made another orbit, and at last saw flak bursting to the north-west at the same height as myself; flew that way and spotted a wave of 88s coming through it towards me, rather difficult to distinguish among the black bursts. Thought of making a head-on attack, but decided it would be better to dive with them. As I reached them the 88s began to stuff their noses down, one after the other, in their bombing-dives; I could see a couple of 109s away to the south, but didn't think they'd worry me, hoped perhaps they hadn't seen me. I turned round to join the stream, picked up my 88 and tucked myself in behind him, following him in his 60° dive; was just laying my sight on him when a 109 came in from the south, firing hard, and I had to break towards him.

My memory of the next minutes is very blurred; I had the impression of at least four, I think six, attacking in the most determined way I'd ever experienced, from every direction; most 109s make off after delivering one attack, but these came back repeatedly and I should say each fired once at least. I managed to take them all head-on or on the beam and felt no hits in the aircraft.

If they had synchronised their attacks I think they must have got me, but they seemed to come down in turn and this just gave me time to deal with each individually; as soon as one had been evaded I'd look round and there would be another one attacking, sometimes already firing. It was a non-stop performance and I've no idea how long it lasted, it might have been five minutes, it might have been fifteen. At the start I lost height by design, hoping the barrage would make them shy, but soon this became sheer necessity; at first I could catch glimpses of the tail-end 88s diving past and there was a good deal of flak, later both disappeared and left me alone with the 109s. There was no chance to look at the clock, but I must have been doing 300 or more most of the time, to judge by the weight of the controls. I had my feet on the g-pedals and was kicking the aircraft about with all my strength whenever they fired; from first to last I was too hard pressed to get a shot back at any of them. Gradually I began to tire and wondered how much longer I could keep it up; remember thinking they were bound to get me if they persisted and speculated whether I should have any chance of jumping out at that speed. As I tired, the controls seemed to grow heavier and heavier, and the physical effects of the g more and more crushing. I can remember I heard myself saying 'God' once and later 'Christ', but the words were wrung out of me and sounded more like groans than oaths. I felt no exaltation in hard fight, had no time to think romantic thoughts of fighting to a finish. I didn't even realise consciously that I was fighting for my life, but must have known it subconsciously. All I felt was an increasing desperation as I tried.

At last I must have grown too ham-handed in a turn and the machine spun; it wasn't intentional, but it was the best thing that could have happened. Normally I hate it, but this time I felt rather smug, knowing that I made a hopeless target; it occurred to me that anyone watching from the shore would probably believe me shot down. Pulled out at 2,000 feet, looked all round carefully and found I was alone, so flew inland towards Luqa. Now that it was all over I felt absolutely exhausted; there was no hope of climbing up to bomber height again in time to do any good; decided I'd better land quickly before the circuit-strafers arrived.

Over Luqa at 1,500 feet I saw two 109s at the same height to the south; they came in to attack and I pulled over the top of them as the leader opened fire and then came down behind No 2. He was about 350 yards away and I hoped I should get a shot at him, but I had to keep watching four other aircraft behind me – they may have been friendly, but I wasn't taking any risks – and as he dived downwards I lost sight of him against the ground. I was too tired to feel very sorry. Then Woodie's voice came through the R/T asking any aircraft that could to cover the landing of a damaged Spit at Takali. At first I was still too exhausted to comply, even the effort of turning the R/T switch over to transmit seemed too much to attempt, but when the message was repeated I made the effort and said I'd do so, thinking at the time what a broken reed I'd be if anything attacked. After watching him crash-land at Takali I landed myself at Luqa. I hadn't believed it possible that you could exhaust yourself so much in an aircraft, and wondered rather glumly why I always had to take these beatings; so far this week to earn one five-second burst at an 88 I've twice been the target for half a dozen 109s and once been blown up by a bomb. However it was cheering to find that the machine hadn't a hole in it anywhere.

The paper to-day says that the Luftwaffe is desperately short of fighters: that's nice to know anyway.

IX

Sunday 26.4.42

Usual raids. Heard that a Hurricane which attempted the same lone-wolf tactics as I did yesterday wasn't so lucky; he got jumped by a number of 109s and one of them got him.

I remember sitting in our little room overlooking the courtyard and hearing someone outside whistle 'Over the Rainbow'. The tune and the bright, hot sunshine took me back to Hastings on those bright, hot days two years before when France had crumbled away. I recalled my feelings at that time and was surprised to find how much they had changed in the interval.

The war had obsessed me for eighteen months before it had broken out. I had grown up in the belief that there would never be another and had treated the primitive military training given at school, like the rest of that generation, with the exasperated acceptance accorded to a traditional obligation. After leaving school I had put it gratefully behind me, and had regarded those who did not do the same as not the least remarkable of the cranks produced by a University notorious for them. Indeed I had earlier rejected all idea of a career in any of the fighting services because the only object and justification of such a life was a war, and everyone knew there would never be another.

This was the period when Hitler was still little bigger than a man's hand, and Englishman and German knew and liked the other. I remembered a beery evening in Frankfurt in 1933 when a huge German and I had talked politics; he had spat on the floor with some ceremony at every mention of France and owlishly wrung my hand whenever England was spoken of. The next year there had been a slight change of attitude, but it had been on the side of the Germans I had met, not mine, and I put it down to the new régime. The Luftwaffe had just been publicly announced, and it was not imagination when I thought the glove nó longer felt like pure velvet. But I was still pro-German and blushed for myself when reminded that, as a small boy of eleven, I had sweepingly and stubbornly insisted to the Swiss-Tyrolese family with whom I had spent a year that I disliked all Germans. That was before I had even met any, and I thought what an insular and uncivilised little villain I must have been.

I did not visit Germany again for three and a half years. When I returned it was early in 1938, less than a month before the Anschluss, and I sensed the change immediately. It was Fastnacht, and I was alone, so I stayed in a little pub on the river at Heidelberg – the *Vier Jahreszeiten* – and soon made friends with the people who came in to celebrate the season. They were friendly and jolly, and the older ones were unchanged, but among the younger generation I noticed a difference. There was everywhere shown an interest in England and things English; it made you feel they were measuring you up.

The son of the house was a boy of nineteen and I had some long talks with him. We argued about the question of colonies, which was prominent at that time, and I was shaken, not so much when he said that he supposed it meant war if England refused to give up Germany's former possessions, as by his calm acceptance of the probability and his ability to shut his mind to any argument if it conflicted with what he had been taught and what he clearly wanted to believe. Yet he was a pleasant, well-mannered boy, with something almost effeminate about him in some ways, and he had told me he had no use for the Party toughs.

Late one night, when we were all full of beer, another of these Germans who, to judge by his assumed superiority over the others and his hints of secret information, was probably a party-member, said that Prague would soon be German. I was not the only one to scoff, but I accepted a bet with him and as the result of it I now owe him one mark. At that time the suggestion seemed preposterous; a month later Austria had succumbed and I began to see what was happening.

It was not until Prague was occupied a year afterwards that I finally admitted to myself that war was inevitable, yet looking back I should say that my whole outlook changed from the time of my visit to Heidelberg. Germany was believed to be re-arming fast, but nothing was known for certain, and in the Palatinate and Rhineland there was no evidence that anything out of the ordinary was going forward. Nevertheless, I came home with a very vivid impression of Germany's new strength and spirit, and one thing left a deeper mark than any other. It was the pictures I saw of the Luftwaffe's new aeroplanes; I did not even know what they were, but I could see from their lines how fast and modern they must be, and our vulnerability to air-attack – opposing those sleek monoplanes with heavily-braced biplane-fighters – became almost an obsession with me.

When war broke out I was out in the African bush. October 1st came and went without my hearing anything, and I was beginning to grow hopeful, when a tired runner arrived at my camp one evening with a single envelope. As soon as I saw it I knew what had happened; it was too small to be my usual mail package, and could be nothing else.

It is difficult to recapture or analyse the confused feelings of those days. Since my leave I had watched the menace of Germany grow more and more threatening, and from the time of the Munich crisis it had monopolised my interest and attention in a way my work no longer could. I felt it impossible to carry on as before with my job; everything we were doing in Africa would be swept away at a stroke if there was a war and we lost it. Germany had to be beaten if there was to be a future for anything; to go on working and ignore Germany was to build on sand. Feeling like this it was almost with relief that I read that war had at last come.

I suppose the exile feels more strongly than anyone that he must go to his country's help. The French catch the spirit of this instinct best with their phrase '*la patrie en danger*'; you sense that it is a rallying-call which will cross ocean or desert, bridge all differences and admit no denial. It was in that way that it affected me. I felt a compelling urgency to give my service and I wanted to fly, both because I felt certain that the air would be the decisive element, and because I believed it would give me the best opportunities; that it was dangerous only suited my mood.

I was glad that the cause was a good one; it would be comforting to know you were fighting for something which conscience approved. Yet such was the irrational urgency which I felt that even if the cause had been much less worthy I doubt whether I should have behaved differently. Probably long stretches of loneliness had made me more susceptible to the disease than most people.

The first six months of war produced only bewilderment and frustration, and by the spring I had almost accepted what seemed to be the common view that the French and British regulars would be enough to crush this upstart Germany. I had gone home on leave, learnt to fly, secured my release from my ordinary work, and was beginning to think I had made a fool of myself, when the Norwegian campaign opened and I knew I had been right.

During the Battles of France and Britain I was under training, first on the south coast and later near London. I found my loyalty to and affection for the country increased with the danger. It also became more unquestioning, because I chose to see only the national virtues, and closed my eyes to the vices. The way in which the ordinary man rose to face the crisis made this easy: there was staunchness, hard work and a friendliness such as I had never seen. Navvies building gun-posts worked as never before, and as Air Force cadets we had only to raise our hands on the roads to be given lifts in the sleekest or most crowded cars.

After the crisis I became gradually disillusioned. I heard a young woman – very wealthy and not in any of the services – complain bitterly because one of her two houses had been commandeered for refugees. I saw navvies, drawing as much or more pay for their safe unskilled work as air-crews, idling their time away. I tried to get a lift, while wearing uniform, from Kidlington to Oxford, and was ignored by at least eight cars which could have given it to me, and finally travelled gratefully on the petrol-bowser. I heard the current stories of workers who drew their double wages for Sunday attendance and took their day off later in the week; of others who stopped work rather than pay income-tax. I became a victim of the apparently almost universal petty thieving. Finally, Greece, Crete and Singapore, coming after Norway and Dunkirk, helped to destroy the memory of the *Rawalpindi, Jervis Bay* and the defence of Calais.

I began to realise that Arthur Bryant's England was dead. Here and there it still survived; in the towns when they were subjected to the Luftwaffe's blitzes and in the friendliness of village life something of the old spirit was left, but there were too many inconsistencies. I found I too had changed. The casualness with which we muddled through our wars had always seemed rather engagingly amateur; now, when matched against German efficiency, it became a terrible example of national apathy. The song – 'We're gonna hang out the washing on the Siegfried Line' – had once seemed pleasantly iconoclastic; now it sounded childish, a symbol of that smugness which ignored present reality and fed its belief in national pre-eminence on half-digested and often tendentious history.

I had discovered at Oxford that I liked Americans and people from the Dominions and had as much in common with them as with other Englishmen. Squadron life had shown me that, but for the language difficulty, the same could be true in the case of Czechs and Poles. The disillusionment I had felt was only to be expected; it was common to the men who had done the fighting in the last war. In 1940 I had wanted to help the country and I suppose I had whitewashed it in my mind to avoid being distracted by its blemishes; now I saw that there were a few people and many factors in the national life which were not worth saving. What was unexpected was that in the place of what had died there sprang up something new.

In 1940 America had stood aside watching the war with suspicion. We had been fighting for existence and the most we could have hoped from victory would have been the liberation of Europe; there was no prospect, since the war was then confined to Europe, of a world settlement when it was over. Now, with the United States, Russia and China as allies, and the third villain in the open against us, there was every hope of a peace worth making. The English-speaking peoples had their faults, but they had conscience and common decency in larger measure than most other people, and a world disarmed and dominated by them, in conjunction with their two large and many small allies, gave promise of better things than any other I could imagine.

I knew this was a more worthy cause than the one which had drawn me two years before, and I tried to recall the unthinking devotion I had then felt, but failed. The rapture and sense of dedication had gone, and my interest in other things had revived. I supposed this was because of eighteen months of squadron life; possibly it was too high-geared a sentiment to survive two years of war; or perhaps the fighting I had experienced had been enough to appease my frustrated desire to serve. I could not be sure; I only knew I was not indifferent to life as I had once been.

I realised too, that I had been growing over-introspective in the last days. In the intervals of flying there was nothing to do but think; I had tried to fix my mind on other things, but found it increasingly difficult to do so. It was bad enough, when you thought all day, but now I was beginning to sleep irregularly and to lie awake at night too. From chance remarks dropped by the others I think they were in the same case, but of course no-one would admit. This is the sort of thing you dare not admit even to yourself, for fear that you might crumble and throw your hand in.

I had always had a feeling that I should survive the war, but recently I had found myself weighing it up, over and over again, in an attempt to determine its validity. At various times I had had other similar feelings; some had been trivial, such for instance that I should win a race at school, while others had been convictions which affected and even determined the course of my life. With one exception events had always proved me right. When I had felt that I was to win that race the belief was not induced by the fact that I was faster than my opponents; I simply felt that fate would allow me to win it. And yet, considering it critically now, I had to admit that I had trained in a Spartan way and that it might have been the determination born of the conviction, not the unforeseen power behind it, which had proved me right.

I had experienced those convictions often enough to believe that I had some power to sense the future where it affected me. Moreover I had been banged on the head two or three times so hard that for some minutes afterwards I had felt that everything that was happening was a repetition of what had happened to me before. I knew that there was a scientific explanation for this phenomenon, but the experience tended to strengthen my belief that the future was not divided from the present by an impenetrable wall.

Yet even if the future cast a shadow into the present I still could not be certain that I had the power to see and interpret it correctly. I had only once been wrong, but this was the most clear-cut case of all, and at the time I had felt bitter disappointment. Now I wondered whether the belief in my survival was another illusion, another prank played by fate at my expense.

I found that with this scepticism came doubts which made me want to exercise this faculty, if I had it, afresh. I kept trying to stretch my spiritual antennae into the future to sense whether anything lay ahead. Sometimes my old life before the war, and even England and my career in the Service there, seemed so remote, and a return to it so unlikely, that it made me think that nothing further was in store for me. It was like hearing the rapids ahead; I told myself not to be a bloody fool, that I was allowing my imagination to riot; but I was fascinated and could not abandon these speculations.

Bound up with them was the problem of predestination. On the whole I found it more comfortable to believe that if you were to die you would die, and if you were to survive you would survive. When the difference between a cannon shell over your head and a cannon shell in the cockpit represented an immeasurably short space on a German reflector-sight or an immeasurably short time in a German head, it was beginning to be terrifying to believe that your fate depended on your own vigilance, and yet terrible to think of it in the blind capricious hands of chance. There was comfort in the thought of immutable laws – it removed the fever and the fret – if you did not reflect that you were moving inexorably towards an end which might be near and could be so hideous.

I kept wondering what sort of mood I should wake up in if I was to be killed later in the day, whether morose or over-confident, nervous or expectant, with foreboding or at peace. I had always noticed that the highest expectations preceded the greatest falls, and I was deeply suspicious of any exalted moods. I wondered how much longer I could continue to see every 109 which attacked me in time to evade and spoil his shot, and how many more times I could be shot up without being shot down. I never paused to think what death meant and was indifferent whether it led to extinction or another life; I did not want to die and I had a good reason for wanting to live. Moreover I had seen too many aircraft crash not to be afraid of dying.

I remembered that when we had first arrived the CO had told the

AOC that we should fight to the last aircraft, and that I had felt pleased and rather heroic. I knew that I did not feel heroic any more and wondered whether I could still fight to the end; on the whole I thought I could, but felt no certainty. What I did know was that the only thing which made me go on, in the face of everything, was not devotion to a theory or ideal, but a determination to satisfy my own self-respect by doing what I had set out to do. But I wished I could see some end to it all.

I decided that I must be getting rattled and needed a rest; I hoped it was the reaction to a tough week and that it would pass.

X

Monday 27.4.42

Bren told me to-day that he had an experience similar to mine. He'd found himself alone, with a wave of 88s plus 109 escort coming towards him; had decided it would be necessary to tackle the 109s first, so attacked four of them and destroyed one at once, whereupon the other three had put their noses down and vanished; he'd then had leisure to deal with the 88s and had got one of these as well. That seemed simple and sound, and made me wonder why I always had to do things the hard way. Bren added that he'd shot the wing right off his 109; the other day Daddo-Langlois of 249 made a head-on attack on another, both broke too late and they met wing to wing; the 109's was sliced clean through, but the Spit had been able to fly home and land. It's nice to know that our aircraft are that much tougher than theirs.

Tuesday 28.4.42

Came to readiness at Luqa at dawn with four aircraft. Shorty's machine went unserviceable, so I only had Chris and a 601 pilot with me when we scrambled at 0740; with four Hurricanes we made up the striking force, while two other Spits acted as aerodrome defence. Dislike mixed formations, so we acted independently. I led them south in the same way as last time and we reached 22,000 feet uneventfully; there was a thin layer of cloud at 21,000 feet and when Woodie told us to come in it made a fine protective ceiling, under which we felt very snug. Arrived over Grand Harbour and saw 88s below us, diving on it from the north; followed them down, but found we were slightly too late to catch them comfortably, so pulled out at 8,000 feet and re-formed. The 601 pilot broke away and looked as if he meant to land – some trouble we supposed – but Chris and I began to orbit and presently sighted Stukas, diving in a stream, all perpendicularly, and pulling out towards the east. Chose my man, manoeuvred to a position astern and underneath, took a last look round while waiting for the range to close, more from habit than in expectation of seeing anything, and was surprised to find an aircraft behind me firing. Thought, My God, 109; then saw its Stuka undercart and thought, Well, it can't be firing; yet it undoubtedly was, so thought, Perhaps it's a 109 after all; looked again and made sure of both the tracer and the undercart and finally admitted that it was a Stuka and that it was attacking me. Pulled out of line, feeling rather as if I'd been charged by an outraged ewe. Was amazed to find him following me round in the turn; not very perturbed, perhaps, because I could see that his deflection was far too small, but I kept thinking 'the intrepid bastard.' I should like to hear the line he's shooting in his mess to-night; feel he's justified, too.

Returned to the procession, placed myself below and astern another one and opened fire with two cannon at 250 yards in an interrupted five-second burst. I saw strikes and he began to take most violent evasive action; I closed right in until I'd lost him under my nose. Dropped a wing to look at him and thought I saw a thin white stream of glycol-vapour, but wasn't certain. I'd found him half-way between Luqa and Valetta at 6,000 feet, and we were now off Grand Harbour at 1,500. I dived on him again and repeated the attack with the same result, before two 109s left the off-shore patrol and made me break off; it was no use going on, I could see others behind them. Landed without incident. This was a lesson to me in how effective really violent evasive action can be; normally I shouldn't have fired while the target was being thrown about, but waited my opportunity, but here the time-element is too important for such refinements and it's essential to fire quickly to fire at all. All the same felt bitterly disappointed in my shooting, after all the time I've spent in practice.

Wednesday April 29 – Sunday May 3
Raids were on a much lighter scale than usual. For the first time since our arrival we saw Italian bombers; on Wednesday five BR 20s flew over at 22,000 feet from west to east and attempted some high-level bombing of Luqa, but missed their target. The ack-ack followed them right across the island, leaving a milky-way in their

track against the familiar blue background; there seemed to be bursts all round them, but not hits, and they maintained perfect formation. Next time they came over they brought their own fighter-escort, reinforced by 109s, and again on their third visit. The Italian fighters flew huddled together, as if for protection, in three groups; they were so close together that the only one who could possibly have kept a look-out was the leader of each bunch, the others must have had their eyes glued to each others' wing-tips; it was so ludicrous that someone was heard to offer a beer to the first Spit to attach himself to their formation without being noticed. They must have been terribly inexperienced, it was a pity we hadn't anything airborne. Once they seemed to act as cover for the bombers, and once to be on their own; as close escort they were too far behind to be effective, and when they operated independently they seemed more interested in Gozo, which they patrolled busily, than in Grand Harbour, where the action was taking place.

There are rumours that the recco Spit found 50 fewer 88s and 30 fewer 109s in Sicily; we seemed to have heard that story before; but it may be significant that the Eyeties are beginning to take a hand. There are still plenty of Huns coming over. Jimmie got a 109 probable and Chris got an 88 probable; Chris stayed a shade too long behind his and got shot up by a 109, splinters in his hand and backside, but nothing serious.

The CO has been made a Wing-Co. and taken over Takali from Satchell, who goes to Air HQ; Bart takes over the squadron. Satchell had his reward before he went; he has manned twin-Brownings on the ground in practically every raid and banged intrepidly away at everything, whether it was in range or not and whether it was bombing him or not; the other day he caught a 109 doing some circuit-strafing and shot it down.

Heard that the estimated weight of bombs dropped on the island in April was 6,700 tons, this is half as much again as my reckoning.

Went into town with Australia and Old Bailey, and had some drinks in Tony's bar in Sliema and then lunch in the most fly-blown joint I've ever visited; the food, however, was surprisingly good. Later visited St John's Cathedral; the verger was asleep, but a friendly copper insisted on waking him and when he found we were pilots he didn't seem to mind a bit. Thought the most striking thing

(*Right*) 'Daddo-L' – Raoul Daddo-Langlois.

(*Below*) 'Bren' – Paul Brennan.

was the pavement made up of the tombs of the Knights; beautiful workmanship, flush-riveting is nothing to it. Mosaics are so often spoilt by garish or ill-matched colours, these were restrained and well-harmonised. One tomb attracted our attention; it showed the conventional figure of Death dominating the world, with the inscription:-

Hora venit ejus
Veniet et tua

Unnecessarily blunt, we thought.

Decided it was time that I took a rest; tried to persuade Jimmie to come with me, but he was due to fly next day and was feeling ambitious, so Old Bailey and I went to St Paul's Bay together; bathed there in the afternoon and read *Pickwick*.

Monday-Tuesday May 4-5
Amused by one suggestion in the book at the rest camp: that the people opposite, in the interest of war-weary pilots, be requested to erase the number of their house. Looked across the road and it was 109. Nice to escape for a couple of days, but we had to cut the visit short when Bart phoned that we must all go to Luqa for a conference dealing with the reinforcements which were expected at the end of the week. Hitch-hiked back to the mess for lunch and heard that MacQueen had been shot down; apparently his R/T had failed and he had never heard his No 2's warning; a 109, which was darting home northward alone, pulled up underneath him and gave him a burst in passing. Those who were watching saw cannon-strikes and say that he appeared to lose and then regain control, but he must have been hit himself, because, after straightening out, his aircraft went down again and never recovered.

Poor Mac, he was the most likeable and modest person; also one of the most successful, with seven confirmed plus probables in the two months he'd been here. He'd had one narrow escape, after following an 88 too far, when six 109s jumped him out at sea; in his evasive action his motor had cut out and at 1,000 feet he'd tried to bale out, but had been unable to open or jettison his hood; he'd given himself up as lost, and then at 200 feet his engine, for no reason, had cut in again and brought him safely home. Even then, and I think on all his other flights, neither he nor his machine had been hit, and now a casual burst from a 109, which was much more interested in getting home than in fighting, proved fatal. It's difficult to follow. When someone is shot down you shut your mind to it and carry on as if he was away on leave. It was only when I saw that MacQueen's bed, which stood opposite the door, and all his personal kit, including a photograph of a girl, had been taken away, that it came home to me what had happened.

Heard Douglas of 603 describe how he'd attacked a Stuka and shot the whole glass-house off it; as he'd overrun it he'd passed within a few feet and had been able to see the gunner sprawling over the back of the cockpit, one arm over the side, headless. They wouldn't give him more than a damaged.

Knew Bart and Jimmie had done a lot of readiness lately, so offered to take over at dawn; Florida and Tiger would go on with me.

Wednesday 6.5.42
Came to readiness at dawn, three of us and four from 603; only six machines serviceable, so decided that 603 should provide the striking force with four aircraft, and Tiger and I should act as aerodrome defence. The morning seemed to go very slowly until we were finally scrambled at 1100; took Tiger well south and climbed to 15,000 feet. This was his first flight here; at first, he kept station well, but gradually began to lag behind; I called him twice on the R/T and throttled back, but no response. Heard Woodie tell 603 to come in and knew our turn wouldn't be long, so began to edge in toward Gozo.

There were big cumulus clouds over the island at 3-5,000 feet, but above these and round them the weather was as brilliant as usual. At last Woodie told us to come in too; R/T was so indistinct that I had to ask him to repeat the message twice before I was certain; flew towards the sun from the north-west, gradually losing height and keeping a very careful look-out, but saw nothing. Woodie told us that there were 109s over Halfar making a nuisance of themselves, so I began to go down in wide spirals. Wished Tiger would keep up; he'd dropped so far behind that if anything jumped him I shouldn't even see it, let alone be able to help. Suddenly noticed four 109s directly below, flying north in pairs line astern; they were crossing from starboard to port, so I waggled my wings to try to bring Tiger up and dived on them. Came up behind the second pair and slightly below, strongly tempted to open fire prematurely, but held it. I kept thinking, 'Surely they must have seen me by now,' but apparently they hadn't, all four flew on straight and level; took a last look behind me and saw only Tiger, still a long way behind.

At last decided that the range had closed and opened fire on the starboard man of the second pair. My machine immediately began to yaw badly; hell's bloody bells, only the port cannon firing; gave him three seconds and watched for results: black smoke came back, but I couldn't be sure whether I'd hit him or if he was pulling his plug. There was no time to speculate, the leading pair seemed to have noticed nothing and were flying on as before, but the companion of the one I'd fired at pulled out from his position on the port side, right across my bows, and began to climb to starboard. I followed him and fired two 2-second bursts with the one cannon and then held my fire, thinking that I should have enough overtaking speed to close in to point-blank range; soon discovered I was wrong, he ran right away from me on the climb and got out of range.

In the meantime I'd been keeping an eye on the first one; he turned and began to head back south, when Tiger came up from underneath, delivered a climbing attack and got on his tail. I thought I must have hit him with my first burst for Tiger to have caught him so quickly. They both turned east and passed quite close to me; the 109 was obviously in trouble, it was flying slowly and only making gentle turns for evasive action. Looking back I wish now that I'd helped to polish him off, but at the same time the obvious course seemed to be to leave him to Tiger and try to get his boy friend. Set off south in pursuit of the other, saw him dive slightly and then climb, not into the sun, but near it. I pulled up too and lost sight of him momentarily in a turn, then glanced round and happened to see another 109 sneaking up on me from the west; had no idea where he'd come from, but he looked dangerous, so I wrenched the aircraft round to port to give him a full deflection shot and, as he opened fire, kicked on bottom rudder and stuffed the nose down. I must have overdone it with the stick, because the negative g made the engine cut; I watched him pass round behind me in a left-hand turn and dive away northward towards a big cumulus cloud below. Don't know why it was, whether disappointment at having had and lost a good attacking position without a confirmed success, or just being brassed-off at serving as a target for 109s without firing back at them. But although I knew there was another one behind me, I never gave it a thought but dived after this new one; gave him a 2-3 second burst – still only one cannon firing – before he reached cloud cover, then took a quick and guilty glance over my left shoulder, but saw nothing.

Next instant, without warning, bang, bang, bang, I could hear and feel three cannon-shells exploding in the bottom of my machine. I remember instinctively kicking on the rudder after the first explosion and feeling how futile it was as the other two followed in quick succession, as quickly as you can say three words, and then experiencing that sensation of insignificance and resignation that comes when you are suddenly overtaken by fate; I remember also that I realised that the aircraft was on fire. Then there is a gap in my memory which I still don't fully understand; it can't have lasted more than two or three seconds, and the most likely explanation seems to be that when it was hit the machine did something of its own accord so violent that I was momentarily blacked out. Alternatively my head may have hit part of the cockpit – a deep gash was afterward found under my hair – and I may have been knocked out. My only recollection is a hazy one of putting the stick forward and correcting a spin, but the speed must already have been 270-300 and the nose was down, so it can't have been that.

When full consciousness returned, I found myself still in the seat, squirming this way and that against the straps, but making no effort to undo the harness and get out, with a great flame rushing up from the bottom of the cockpit and being drawn past my face by the suction of the slip-stream. My first thought was that this time it was certainly the end and that there must have been some mistake, because I wasn't supposed to die. The fire prevented me from seeing anything outside the aircraft, but I could tell by feel that it was diving very steeply and fast and, after being blacked out for those few moments, I must have imagined I was nearer the ground than I actually was. After the last experience I never thought I should be able to escape this time.

I can remember I noticed a curious smell; I don't know whether it was something burning, or me being burnt; it was not so much unpleasant as entirely strange to me, and it was this, not heat or pain, which was the most forcible physical sensation. I found afterwards that my legs had been peppered by cannon-splinters, but I never felt them at the time. No past life flashed before me, I think things happen too quickly in the air for this to be possible; I only remember that everything was red, that I felt this terrible flame was robbing me of the power to think, and that I knew that if I lost my head it would destroy me. I thought of what was waiting a few hundred or a few thousand feet below, I didn't know which, that terrible crash and burst of flame. In the meantime I'd very deliberately pulled out the locking-pin of the harness; I knew I couldn't afford to fumble with it and remember I shaded my eyes with my left arm and looked down so as to make sure; then half stood in the cockpit, decided there was no time to try to take my helmet off and it would have to be risked, kicked the stick forward as far as I could, felt the helmet and mask parting, and was shot forward into the air. The aircraft was diving so fast that I might have been an arrow and it a tautened bow. I must have passed out at once, I don't even remember pulling the rip-cord and have no memory of the chute opening or of the descent, only hitting the ground, then more oblivion.

I began to come round as the first Tommies arrived; they helped me to unbuckle the chute and soon had me on a stretcher. I don't know where they took me, I had a cloth over my head and was taking little interest; I remember hearing the sympathetic wailing of a crowd of Maltese and a voice saying: 'Is he dead?' I wanted to say, 'No bloody fear,' or something like that, but shirked the effort, it was so much easier to keep absolutely still; my right leg was numb now, and face and arms had grown pretty painful. We arrived at some sort of barrack-room and a medical orderly put a dressing on my left knee, which was bleeding from a splinter wound. After what seemed a long wait an ambulance arrived; by this time I had begun to suffer from violent shivering-fits and my face and arms were growing hotter and hotter and steadily more painful. I lay there wondering whether I should lose my eyesight, and how much my face would be disfigured.

At last we reached the hospital; I was given a shot of morphia, which seemed to have no effect, and ringed round with the most comforting hot-water-bottles, my clothes were cut away to a chorus of reassuring remarks – a bit too reassuring, I thought – and I was taken first to the X-ray room and then to the theatre. There I was given a shot in the leg and told to count slowly; I got to 25 without difficulty and felt the stuff reach my head, just managed to say 26 and was gone before I could even think of 27.

When I awoke the shivering fits had left me, arms and face were buried in bandages, and I was fairly comfortable in bed.

I introduced myself to the other patients whom I could hear in the ward, and learnt that they were two naval and one army officer. I did not then know what their injuries were, but discovered later that they were all bomb casualties, one with an injured spine, one a compound fracture of the thigh, and the third an amputated leg. I didn't see them for nearly a fortnight, but their voices sounded kind and sympathetic and the mental pictures of them which I had formed proved to be unusually accurate.

I found I was very thirsty and conceived an overmastering craving for an apple, not an ordinary one, but a Cox's Orange Pippin from the garden at Easterton. Failing that, I wanted a beer, but both were not only forbidden but unobtainable, and I had to be content with water. This was given to me in a feeder with a rubber extension on the spout; my lips felt like two over-done banana-fritters and an orderly therefore had to spill the water into my mouth drop by drop.

It hadn't occurred to me that as it grew dark the little light which penetrated my bandages would gradually drain away; I only suddenly realised that I was in deeper darkness than I had ever known. I tried to open my eyes, but could not, and was not sure whether it was the weight of the bandages or whether the lids were stuck together. Before I had been able to think dispassionately of possible blindness; now I almost lost control of myself in a furious impulse to tear my bandages off, and push my lids open. Bit by bit I was able to fight it back and drill myself into resignation.

Next morning Colonel Mitchell came to change my dressings. The bandages and lint were peeled off and I was told to open my eyes if I could; I found I could not. When the lids had been further cleaned it was possible to force them apart and I looked up to see, in poor focus, a section of distempered wall with two faces in front of it, peering anxiously into mine. That was all I saw, for two minutes every day, for nearly a fortnight; yet, in spite of the pain which accompanied it, this was a treat to which I looked forward.

My eyes were giving off a heavy liquid which had to be cleaned away each time the dressings were changed. At first the process was not very painful, but as my eyelids healed it became, increasingly, an ordeal which I dreaded. If I hadn't believed Colonel Mitchell to be a humane man I should have thought that he was scouring out my sockets with wire-wool.

For the rest, my face gave little trouble and healed astonishingly quickly. My arms proved more troublesome. The worst burns were at the elbow and these proved painful if any of the weight of the arm rested on them; yet it was difficult to lie face upward without doing this and the dressings on my face precluded any other position. For a week, until I had evolved some sort of technique, I spent restless days and almost sleepless nights.

Every three or four hours the face-dressings were drenched in a saline solution; this not only had healing qualities of its own but prevented the lint from sticking to my flesh. The risk of infection was too great for similar applications to the arms to be allowed; a saline bath inside a length of mackintosh bound round my arm was therefore improvised, but sooner or later the water always seeped away at wrist or shoulder and the arm dressings seldom remained saturated like those on my face. The removal of these dressings after they had dried on, and stuck to, the flesh was, with the cleansing of my eyes, the principal source of pain. I felt sorry for myself and I found out the extent of the injuries of the other men in the ward; then I saw how much I had to be thankful for.

For the first day I was allowed only water; on the second, fruit; by the third I was on a light diet. Feeding was a problem because of the bandages and my negroid lips; the orderlies patiently forked the solids and poured the liquids into me and as time went on I was able to help myself more and more.

Colonel Mitchell had told me to try not to remember what had happened, but it was impossible not to, and I ran through the action again and again in my mind; I tried to think what had induced me to dive after that 109 when I'd known that another was behind me. Before, I'd always been so sensitive of my tail, yet then I'd accepted an unjustifiable risk; I couldn't explain it. Then I would fight all the other engagements over again. It was the failures, not the successes, that I dwelt on; I thought especially of the Stuka I had let through my fingers the week before, and told myself dozens of times how I ought to have dealt with him, then of that 88 which I had failed to polish off, and so back to the last engagement, and I would curse myself again for having been such a bloody fool.

Although I thought about them so much, I felt I never wanted to see an aeroplane again and that I could never bring myself to do any more flying; this feeling was so strong that at times I found myself hoping that my eyes would have suffered too much for me to be passed fit for flying. If this failed, I wondered how I could decently escape – whether I could persuade the Colonial Office to ask for me back again, and whether the RAF would let me go if they did so, or whether the war would be over quickly enough to solve the problem. On the fourth day this aversion modified; I didn't want to fly again, but decided I could if I had to; it was some time before it passed altogether and I continued to feel thankful that I was out of the war for the present.

The boredom, discomfort and pain were nothing beside the beautiful safety of bed and the knowledge that there was no ordeal waiting for me at dawn next day. I felt ashamed of this feeling, and of myself for having it, and I tried to jolt myself out of it, but without effect.

One of the other patients would read the paper to me after breakfast, and that was all my recreation. When it was over, I had to occupy myself with my own thoughts until next morning.

I was surprised to find how my opinions had been affected by my experiences. The case of the pre-war pacifists had always seemed to me before to be overstated, but now I found myself almost in agreement with them. A world in which every man would cultivate his acre of ground became, at this time, the ideal one; that it might be filled with small people, breed small vices, and be as stagnant as a dew-pond seemed not to matter at all; the important thing was that there would be no killing, wounding, disfigurement or pain.

This matter occupied me so much, and I gave it so much thought, that as soon as I could use my eyes again I amused myself by dashing off some essays on the subject to illustrate my new theory that the tendency for human beings to fight each other was fostered by most of the factors of our civilisation, from the emphasis it placed on physical courage to the way in which it taught history.

It was an interesting reflection that, if Hitler had had an operation or accident in 1939, causing him acute pain, he would probably have been unable to loose war on the world.

For a week none of the boys was able to come and see me; I knew it was because the reinforcements had arrived and they were having the long-expected show-down with the Huns. When at the end of that time they were able to visit me they brought good news; the new aircraft had arrived a couple of days after I'd been shot down and the ground organisation, which had been much practised and rehearsed, was masterly; everything had gone off without a hitch and the machines had been in the air again, re-armed and refuelled, within an hour.

Over the week-end a battle had been fought which proved decisive; in those three days 112 enemy aircraft had been destroyed or damaged against negligible losses of our own. These figures seem small compared with the huge totals of 1940, but they represented a high proportion and, coming after four months' attrition, and before the summer campaigns, they proved to be enough for the purpose. The aerial supremacy which we'd lost when the Hun came to Sicily in December had been regained from him and there was an end of the heavy raids.

The Spits had still been outnumbered, but for the first time they found themselves facing reasonable odds, and they took advantage of it. When the five BR 20s came over in their spotless formation, with a close escort of 21 fighters, certainly three and possibly all five of the bombers as well as some of the fighters were destroyed. The Hun, using the same tactics, sent over three 88s with a heavy escort to attack Takali; the Spits jumped them and before they reached the target all three were on fire and all accounted for. In an attempt to sink a ship which had brought ammunition to the island, the Stukas were sent out again; the Grand Harbour barrage at full strength was laid on for them and this made some of them turn back; those who came on were slaughtered by the waiting Spits, ten were certainly, and the remainder probably, destroyed. The ship wasn't touched.

The squadron bag for the period was still under examination, but Goldie alone added five to his score, Florida four and Malaya three; no pilots were lost and only two aircraft. Two-four-nine did as well or better: Hesselyn reached double figures and Pete had a run which carried his score to $14\frac{1}{2}$ – all but two over the island – before he was shot down and killed; he and his No 2 were last seen attacking five 109s, two of which they destroyed. This and one other was the only loss suffered by that squadron.

On the whole luck was on our side. Two pilots of 603, intent on killing the same 109, failed to see one another and collided heavily at about 5,000 feet; both machines disintegrated and their occupants, who still had no idea what had happened, suddenly found themselves in the fresh air with no aircraft; one of them was still sitting on his seat and had to take the locking-pin out of the harness to jettison it before he could open his parachute. The CO of 603 engaged a 109 in a long head-on attack in which both sides fired; as they flashed past each other he saw one wing of the 109 fold up and come-away; the pilot baled out successfully and, with a cannon-shell in his left arm, occupied the next bed to mine. Mike was hit by the return fire of an 88 which he chased out to sea; he felt the engine growing hotter and hotter as he limped home and at the same time it began to lose power. As he crossed the coast his height was only 900 feet and his speed had fallen to 90; he was looking for somewhere to force-land when flames and smoke appeared; luckily he didn't hesitate, but rolled on to his back at once and got safely out. Johnny Plagis, after his No 2 had lost him, chased a reconnaissance machine almost back to Sicily, when he was jumped by eight Macchis; he resorted to the most violent evasive action, but was gradually forced down from 10,000 feet to sea-level, and it seemed to be only a question of time before one of them got him. As he was evading one he saw another coming in on his port-side, so he whipped round to meet it head-on; by this time he was desperate and made no attempt to break away, thinking that if he had to die he would at least take one of the bastards with him. The Italian held on too long and then pulled up so sharply that he must have blacked out; Johnny watched him climb steeply, turn on his back and dive into the sea. He hadn't fired a shot, but the others didn't want to fight any more and left him. Of the many Spits which dived through the Grand Harbour barrage after the bombers, two more were said to have been hit by ack-ack; both the pilots were from 601, one was lost but the other escaped by parachute.

My neighbour the 109 pilot proved to be a Sudeten of Czech antecedents; he knew little English, but I learnt some of his history. He had previously been a Stuka pilot, had managed to get transferred on to fighters, and had made more than a hundred flights over Malta; he claimed five victories, one Blenheim, one Hurricane and three Spits. This was his first theatre of operations, although he'd been in the Luftwaffe more than two years. He seemed to have been assimilated by the Germans and, although he wasn't a party member, or noticeably a Hitler enthusiast, he identified himself with the Herrenvolk. His reasons for doing so were unconvincing and I thought he protested too much; it was probably self-interest. He said supposing we weren't English, but our country had been conquered by the English, wouldn't we fight for England? We said ask the Irish, but he didn't see the point.

Douglas-Hamilton, who had shot him down, visited him in hospital and I couldn't help overhearing their conversation; when asked why 109 pilots shot up dinghies and parachutes he denied that they ever did so and described it as *Schweinerei*. A case had just occurred in which one of our pilots had been picked up in his dinghy, either dead or at the point of death, with a cannon-shell through his neck; he was told of this but refused to believe it. The cases of 1940 were then quoted, but he still said obstinately: '*Das glaub' ich nicht*'. Nor would he admit that our rescue-launch had ever been attacked. I couldn't make up my mind whether he believed what he said or not.

Later he asked me whether I found Italian fighters more or less formidable than 109s; I told him that, as far as I knew, I'd never been engaged with Italians; he laughed a lot, and, when I asked why, explained he was laughing at the Rome radio which always claimed a heavy bag of Spitfires. He didn't care for Sicily, it was too dull and he seemed to hanker after bright lights. In spite of our denials I am sure that he remained convinced that he'd been shot down by a Kittyhawk; he wouldn't have it that it was a Spit, because he'd never been out-climbed by one before.

He was slight in build with fair hair brushed straight back, and I should say not more than twenty-two; he bore his pain bravely, but I never felt comfortable with him. It was difficult not to remember Uher and Brejcha, now both dead, and wonder what he was doing on the other side. I was glad to be moved to another ward soon after his arrival.

One day, before the dressings had been taken off my face, two visitors arrived whose voices I did not recognise; they proved to be the army officers who had picked me up and got the ambulance for me. They told me that when they arrived I was still smouldering gently (this was my Mae West, which had caught fire at the neck) and my face smothered in blood and sand. The first thing I had said was: 'Christ, I thought they'd got me that time'; they added that an enormous crowd of Maltese had turned out and their men had had to keep them back forcibly from the stretcher. The rest of their narrative agreed with what I remembered.

In the new ward I met Julius Caesar; he was a little Italian from Trento, whose radiator had been shot out by a Spit, so that he'd been forced to land his 'Falco' on the island. On the night of his arrival, in the discomfort of a new plaster-cast, he'd embarrassed us all by calling for his 'mama' repeatedly; he seemed to be a timid creature, because later in the week we'd woken up to bellows of '*Luce, luce,*' and, when the light was turned on, had found him crouching in a corner; he went quietly to bed and we supposed it must have been a bad dream. He'd seen service in Libya, but this had been his first flight over Malta. Coming from the Trentino he had no love of Germans; I at once won favour when I told him I knew Bolzano; his girl-friend, an attractive young woman from her photographs, lived there.

I couldn't help both liking and laughing at him. He knew a few words of French and German and with these we would make ourselves understood; if ever I essayed Italian he would repeat the word or phrase musically and wistfully and then say: '*Ah mein schönes*

Land.' For emphasis he had a trick of knocking his knuckles against his plaster-cast and making it ring. Whenever we laughed too much at him he would look pathetic and say, in execrable German: '*Sie lustig, ich nicht lustig.*' He was a gentle soul and how Mussolini hoped to win a war with him was a mystery; I used to amuse myself by drawing a mental comparison between him, as a fighting man, and say Buck McNair. He seldom shaved and when we asked him about this he said a few eccentrics in Italy shaved every day, but twice a week was enough for the rest of them, Regia Aeronautica included. He often said: 'Isn't war terrible?' The first time I heard this I thought my face, just released from its dressings, had prompted the remark, but he repeated it many times.

He seemed to have no hope of victory and little interest in events. The only subject on which he showed any animation was when we discussed the ordeals of bomber as opposed to fighter-pilots. He insisted that fighter pilots were braver; when we put in a word for the bomber-boys, he waved his arms violently to mimic the gyrations of the fighter, then pushed them forward slowly and steadily to indicate the straight and level flight of the bomber. Someone said they supposed he meant that bomber pilots were only chauffeurs; he caught the word and repeated it with relish, and added with withering scorn 'Tramway,' which he pronounced 'Tram-vye'. We gathered from what he said later that this was a case of professional jealousy: his own decorations numbered only four or five, but bomber pilots, to hear him tell it, hadn't an inch to spare, on the left-hand side of their tunics, between shoulder and waist.

Later Kurt turned up, transferred from another hospital. He was cheerful, tried to make himself pleasant, and was far from the serious-minded German of fiction. On the subject of Hitler and the Party he was reticent, but was a sufficiently good German to claim that their news was accurate and to laugh at the suggestion that the BBC could be believed. When he derided our programmes because they were studded with news-bulletins, we told him that these had to be inserted so that thousands of curious and impatient Germans should not be disappointed.

I asked him whether he believed the claims of the leading German fighter-pilots to be correct, for instance Mölders with a score of 115.

He seemed satisfied that they were; when I said I was sure they must be exaggerated he repeated the old story about the need for two witnesses before a victory was confirmed. I asked how many British machines Mölders claimed; he said he didn't know, but Galland had shot down 98, all British; when I told him that I refused to believe that German pilots, who had not had the opportunity of large-scale daylight bombing to swell their scores, could run up numbers three times larger than the best of ours, he regarded me as a wrong-headed and rather unsporting Englishman.

Among other things Kurt showed me a charred snap of MacQueen, the pilot who had shot him down, which he had somehow secured when MacQueen himself was shot down and killed.

In neither of the German prisoners was there the sullenness or arrogance which one heard about at the beginning of the war. Nor did they show any missionary zeal, though I was told that the pilot of an 88 had made an unsuccessful attempt to convert one of the orderlies. He had said that it was a pity that the British misunderstood the Führer, who was kind and gentle and had a heart like a woman's; the orderly agreed gloomily and said he'd met women with hearts like that.

From the point of view of the patient the hospital was a model of what hospitals should be. Colonel Mitchell couldn't take too much trouble with my burns and thanks to his unremitting struggle against infection my face healed by first intention and without disfigurement. Sister Palmer treated me as a friendly lunatic and not as a child with a criminal record; nor did anyone take it upon themselves, as happened later, elsewhere, to tell me that if I hadn't got work to do they had, and everyone couldn't have a nice holiday like me. Moreover, the Code Nightingale had been broken, and washing and bed-making were not carried out with a semi-religious fervour in the hour before dawn. In less than a month I was fit to travel.

On May 29th, after dinner, and a farewell drink with Sister Palmer, I was driven down to Luqa to wait for the big Curtiss Wright. It was a fine night with a bright moon, and it seemed fitting that we should leave from the aerodrome where we had first landed. It was little more than two months ago, but a good deal seemed to have happened since then.

A few days before, Rommel's offensive in Libya had begun; now Wellingtons were returning from a raid on his communications. In the worst days of April we had almost begun to feel that the little we were doing was of no more use than a small gesture of defiance; we could see neither an end to it nor a prospect of success. All the advantages seemed to lie with the enemy: he had the interior lines and could concentrate whatever he pleased against us, while we had limited aerodrome and dispersal facilities, so that whenever reinforcements had arrived they had been swallowed up overnight. It had seemed impossible to maintain more than a handful of fighters against him. The scale of raiding, instead of diminishing, had increased and prisoners of war all agreed that the pressure, if it did not culminate in an invasion, would at least be maintained. There was no respite from the bombing. No relieving force was in sight. The odds, long at the start, lengthened steadily. No end could be foreseen.

Yet the tradition of the Service, forged at such terrible cost by the RFC during the last war, demanded that, so long as there remained an aircraft which would fly, it must be flown and fought, whatever the odds and whatever the price. This had been done. At times it had only been possible to contest the enemy aerial supremacy over the island, but mastery had been stubbornly denied to him, and a steady loss of aircraft had been inflicted.

The lot of the Hurricane pilots had been the hardest: they had taken part in all the bitter defensive battles, had suffered the casualties which the odds against them and the technical inferiority of their machines made inevitable, and yet had been robbed by the obsolescence of their aircraft of the prizes which they might have had.

For the Spitfires the hard fighting was sweetened by substantial successes. At this time the original Spitfire pilots of 249 and 126 Squadrons had already shot down more than one hundred enemy aircraft over and round the island; before the last of them left, this number was increased by half as much again. These were confirmed victories; if the aircraft probably destroyed were included, the final total would be nearly two hundred. The cost was thirteen pilots killed and seven wounded.

The dark days had been those of March and April. In May the situation had changed completely: with the decisive victory, three weeks earlier, aerial supremacy, lost when the Germans had returned to Sicily late in 1941, had been regained. Rommel's offensive had been launched a few days before; yet there, at Luqa, were Wellingtons already operating against his bases and lines of communication. The effort had not, perhaps, been entirely in vain.

Notes to Part One

Page 21
'CO' – Squadron Leader (later, Wing Commander) Edward John Gracie, DFC, who was killed in action 15th February 1944.

'Bart' – Eventually Wing Commander Robert Alexander Barton, OBE DFC (Bar), nicknamed variously 'Sailor' and 'Butch', who retired from RAF service 27th February 1959.

'Mac' – Donald W. McLeod, American, ex-121 'Eagle' Squadron, who died in Connecticut, USA, in October 1946.

'Jimmie' – James E. Peck, America, ex-121 'Eagle' Squadron, killed at Christchurch, 12th April 1944 in accident while flying a Lockheed P-38 Lightning fighter.

Page 31
'Wing-Co' – Wing Commander William Arthur John Satchell, DSO, retired as Group Captain on 1st July 1956.

Page 38
'Woodie' – Group Captain A. B. Woodhall, OBE, retired from RAF on 14th July 1945.

Page 44
'Grant' – Wing Commander Stanley Bernard Grant, DFC (Bar).

Page 49
'Buck McNair' – Eventually Group Captain Robert Wendell McNair, DSO, DFC (Two Bars), RCAF.

Page 50

'Plagis' – Wing Commander John Agorastas Plagis, DSO, DFC (Bar) who became the highest-scoring Rhodesian fighter pilot of the war.

'Nash' – Pilot Officer Peter Alfred Nash, DFC, who scored 13 confirmed victories plus nine others probably destroyed or damaged. Killed in action over Malta on 17th May 1942.

Page 62

'Goldsmith' – Squadron Leader Adrian Philip Goldsmith, DFC, DFM, RAAF who was credited with at least 19 victories. Died 25th March 1961.

'Schade' – Flight Sergeant Patrick Alfred Schade, DFM, credited with 11 victories, born in Malaya.

'Tex' – Hiram Aldine Putnam, American, ex-133 'Eagle' Squadron, who was killed in action over Malta on 21st April 1942.

Page 64

'Australia' – John Henry Eric Bisley, DFC, RAAF.

Page 65

'MacQueen' – Flight Lieutenant Norman Carter MacQueen, DFC, killed in action over Malta on 4th May 1942.

Page 73

'Nippy' – Wing Commander Philip Whaley Ellis Heppell, DFC (Bar).

'West' – Flight Lieutenant Ronald West, DFC (Bar), who scored nine victories.

Page 86

'Buck' – George Andrew Forsyth Buchanan, Rhodesian, scored nine victories. Baled out in combat on 17th May 1942 over Malta but had his parachute shot up by enemy fighter and killed.

Page 100

'Florida' – Reade Tilley, DFC, American, ex-121 'Eagle' Squadron.

'Tiger' – Douglas E. Booth, American, ex-121 Squadron ('Eagle').

Page 122

'Bren' – Virgil Paul Brennan, DFC, DFM, RAAF, killed in flying accident on 13th June 1943. Co-author of *Spitfires Over Malta* (Jarrolds, 1943).

'Daddo-L' – Raoul Daddo-Langlois, DFC

Page 127

'Douglas' – Squadron Leader Lord David Douglas-Hamilton, OC 603 Squadron, AAF, killed in crash of a DH Mosquito on return from a sortie, 2nd August 1944.

Page 135

'Hesselyn' – Ray Brown Hesselyn, MBE, DFM (Bar), RNZAF (later RAF), co-author *Spitfires Over Malta* (Jarrolds, 1943). Died 1965.

PART TWO

D-Day and After

Introduction

by Chaz Bowyer

After hospital treatment for his wounds and burns, Tim Johnston returned to England, and was posted to No 611 Squadron as a supernumerary for flying duties until August 1942 when, as a squadron leader, he was given a staff appointment at HQ Fighter Command. In the interim he had been awarded a DFC on 8th June in recognition of his operations on Malta. In June 1943 Johnston succeeded Squadron Leader E.G.A. Seghers, DFC, as commander of No 165 Squadron, a Spitfire unit based at Ibsley, and remained in this appointment until January 1944 when he was posted to the staff of No 10 Group HQ Fighter Command. In March 1944 came the award of a Bar to his DFC, its citation saying in part; 'He has devoted the utmost energy and enthusiasm in perfecting his squadron as a fighting unit' and crediting him with one enemy aircraft destroyed in combat on 31st December 1943, thereby bringing his official tally of enemy aircraft to four destroyed, three more probably destroyed, and three others claimed as 'damaged'.

In the same month as this latest award Johnston joined the HQ staff of the 2nd Tactical Air Force, then being prepared for the imminent Allied invasion of Normandy, and on 23 May he returned to operations with a posting to command No 66 Squadron at Bognor Regis. Moving its base on 21 June 1944 to Tangmere, 66 Squadron was one of three Spitfire squadrons which comprised No 132 Wing, 2nd TAF, and on 5th September 1944 the wing moved on to the Continent, being based initially at Neufcampville (B.33), then moving to Lille-Nord (B.57) on 11th September, and on to Duerne (B.70) on 25th November. The companion units of 132 Wing were Nos 331 and 332 Squadrons, both Norwegian-manned and commanded respectively by Majors L. Lundsten and W.

Christie; while the overall wing leader was another Norwegian, Lt-Colonel R.A. Berg, DFC, who was succeeded as leader on 16th June 1944 by Major M. Gran, DFC.

The following account, previously unpublished, was written by Tim Johnston to record his actions, thoughts, even philosophies, while commanding No 66 Squadron from D-Day, 6th June 1944, until November 1944 when he was finally rested from operations for the remainder of the war. Having added a Focke Wulf Fw190 destroyed to his tally on 15th June, Johnston returned to the UK in a non-operational post from November 1944 until June 1945, in which month he was 'Mentioned in Despatches' and released from RAFVR service for an 'indefinite period' from 7 June in order to resume his pre-war career in the Colonial Service.

In June 1954 Tim Johnston was awarded an OBE (Civil), and was further honoured with a CMG in 1959, by which time he had finally been released from RAFVR service, with the rank of Wing Commander. In 1960 he became Deputy Governor of the Northern Region of Nigeria, while from 1961-65 he was appointed Director of the Overseas Services Resettlement Bureau. He died on 9th December 1967.

I

At a quarter to three in the morning I was awakened by the sound of aircraft; the stream had already been passing over for some time, apparently, but I had not noticed it. Outside the tent, in the east, there was a faint sign of dawn. In the south-west hung a placid, almost full, moon; the sky, clear except for two distant cloud-banks, was a powdery blue in colour, too bright for the stars to shine through it. The grass underfoot, long and beginning to seed, was damp and fresh with dew; overhead the larks, responding to the glimmer in the east, were already in full song. It was 6th June 1944.

I dressed quickly, without pretence of washing, and carried my parachute out to my aircraft. In that fresh tranquil morning I found some lines of half-forgotten verse running through my head:

> ... in the sky
> The larks, still bravely singing, fly,
> Scarce heard amid the guns below.
> We are the dead. Short days ago ...

The poet had been a Canadian Colonel in the last war, who had been killed soon after writing those premonitory lines. How did they go on?

> To you from failing hands we throw
> The torch; be yours to hold it high;
> If ye break faith with us who die,
> We shall not sleep, though poppies grow
> In Flanders Fields.

It was still dark, but the aircraft had passed, and there was no sound, far or near, but that rapturous larks' song. Had we broken faith?

Between the wars, by our sins of omission perhaps yes, but not now: 6th June 1944 might rank with 1st July 1916 as one of the most dearly-bought dates in history, and our generation suffer losses as catastrophic as did that of the dead Colonel.

I was surprised to find how tranquil and untroubled I was in spirit. The usual dread and sense of foreboding which, ever since I had been shot down, had filled me at the approach of great events, had disappeared. Nor did I feel the cheerful, because ignorant, confidence of two years ago, disposed to welcome opportunities, however dangerous, and make light of odds. These had given way to resignation accompanied by a peace-of-mind which, a year before, I believed I should never recover.

The marquee with the telephones and the pilots' tents was within a hundred yards of the aircraft; having breakfasted and made everything ready, in case we should be needed earlier, there was nothing for us to do but doze until seven o'clock when we would take off on our first patrol. I lay on my bed and listened as formation after formation of aircraft passed overhead. Fighters were beginning to take off from the surrounding airfields and, with stragglers cutting noisily across the corners, were setting course southward; glider-tugs, their night's work complete, were returning in ones and twos from Normandy; medium bombers, British and American, their wings and fuselages picked out in black-and-white markings, passed over in purposeful formations of eighteen and thirty-six; while majestically above them all, disdaining camouflage, the remote, silvery combat wings of Fortresses and Liberators, lit by the pale sunshine of dawn, headed noiselessly towards France.

I went to my tent and lay down, my mind full of the past. For three years we had been flying over this Continental coast, from Brittany to Zeeland, and had had countless opportunities of noting its strength and weakness. From Brest to St Malo it was as forbidding as Cornwall; the western side of the Contentin Peninsula possessed good beaches, but was almost perpetually a lee-shore; Cherbourg was one of the most heavily defended towns in France; the Seine Bay was nearly a hundred miles from our fighter-bases and, in part, under the guns of Le Havre; the Picardy cliffs, from Cap d'Antifer to beyond Le Tréport, were as sheer as Beachy Head. Only between the Somme and the Scheldt were there good, if

The author in 1944. This photograph of the portrait by William Dring has been retouched for official publication.

exposed, beaches and here naturally the enemy had concentrated his defences; behind these shores, too, much of the land was low-lying and susceptible of defence by flooding.

How slowly but inexorably, I thought, had events led up to this day. In 1941 it had been a hazardous undertaking to make even a shallow penetration of the Continent, one which seldom passed without an engagement; in those days the term Festung-Europa had possessed meaning. There had been no great engagements, as during the Battle of Britain, but there began then an enduring, relentless war of attrition between the British and German fighter-forces; with many ups and downs, this was to last for another three years, was to draw in a new generation of pilots on both sides, and was only to be brought to a decision at the cost of grievous casualties.

For us 1941 had been a difficult year. The Hurricane, still in large-scale use, was already obsolescent, for its comparative lack of speed and poor diving qualities made it an ineffective weapon when matched against the improved Me 109. Furthermore, pilots had to accustom themselves to the new type of offensive warfare, with its attendant problem of extricating forces which might be running short of fuel and ammunition from far behind the enemy lines, while mastering the new technique of flying in large formations. Above all, the few veterans of 1940 had to train and guard the new pilots who, with little more than 150 hours' flying-time, were flooding the squadrons.

If the Luftwaffe appeared in 1941 to have effected an astonishing recovery from its defeat the previous year, it had by 1942 become even more confident and aggressive. This summer had been the hardest of all. Not only had all the advantages of the Battle of Britain apparently slipped away from us, but the Germans had seemed capable, thanks to their new fighters, the Fw 190, of parrying our blows in the west while they defeated us in Africa and, in the East, overran the greater part of European Russia.

The air offensive in the west, in spite of heavy losses, had nevertheless been maintained. The war of attrition, which in 1942 had seemed as if it might go against us, suddenly turned in our favour; by 1943 the Luftwaffe was already in decline. A number of factors had contributed to this result: the arrival in Europe of the

American Air Forces, the German defeats in North Africa and the Mediterranean, the development of the Spitfire IX, and the prodigality of the enemy in driving his pilots till they dropped without making adequate provision for their replacement.

During 1943, by pressing our advantage to the utmost, we had succeeded in improving our moral and material preponderance. The number of bombers which could safely be dispatched with a given number of fighters as escorts had been doubled and doubled again. By the beginning of 1944 it had even become possible in some cases to dispense with escorts altogether. Allied bombers and fighters roamed at will over almost the whole of north-west Europe: mastery of air had in fact been won. It was a far cry from the days when one Stirling and a handful of Spitfire squadrons used to fight their way over France, regarding Lille as their deepest target.

During these three years we had come to know the coast of France and the Low Countries more intimately than our own, and scores of times had wondered where the blow would fall. Secrecy and surprise were obviously so vital to success that we no longer even allowed speculation among ourselves. It had only been late on the previous evening, when the landing craft were already under way, and the airborne forces were making their final preparations, that we had been assembled in the old barn which we used as a mess and admitted to the details of the great plan.

We had been told that half-a-dozen capital ships and four thousand other craft would support the landings and that three airborne divisions – the greatest number ever employed – would precede them. We already knew that medium bombers had broken every bridge over the Seine below Paris; we had learned then that they were to do the same in the Loire so as to isolate the battlefield. Feeling as we all did that air-power was the key which would unlock the Continent, we had been most of all impressed by the news that we should form part of a force of 11,000 front-line aircraft, of which 3,000 would be heavy bombers, giving direct or indirect support to the Armies.

Briefing had been conducted undramatically, but the magnitude of the event had impressed itself on everyone present. As we listened to the unfolding of this gigantic undertaking, the barn had been filled with the twittering of a colony of starlings nesting in the roof.

At one point an over-ambitious fledgling, which had made a powered descent from the eaves to the ground, only to find that its climb was inferior to its dive, had to be retrieved, placed on a stick and restored to a worried mother. The burst of laughter, unnaturally loud, which had greeted this interlude, had revealed the tension and excitement which underlay these apparently prosaic proceedings. I noticed how the eyes of the pilots, in particular, were glistening; in three or six months many of them must expect to be killed, but at that moment it was apparent that nothing, no inducement however tempting, would have led any of them to give up his participation. If it is possible to describe the mood of that meeting I should call it controlled exultation.

By morning this feeling had sobered into excitement, tempered by wariness in the face of the unknown conditions which we should be facing.

At seven o'clock we took off and flew by way of St Catherine's Point to Barfleur; the weather had deteriorated since dawn and under 8/10ths of cloud at 4,000 feet the morning looked dour and grey. In the Channel we flew over countless ships of all sizes, the majority of them headed south in convoys, while in the bay of the Seine, anchored off each of the three British and two American beaches, we found further armadas.

The two most striking features in the scene were the immense number of ships present and the apparent lack of activity. There was little enough sign of fighting on the beaches: in the British section some fires were burning, while north-west of M   – an island fortress where Monte Cristo might have been immured – a destroyer had sunk in shallow water, her mast and funnels visible, her ensign still flying.

The two American beaches over which we were to patrol lay in the south-west corner of the bay on either side of the estuary of the Vire; their code names were Utah and Omaha. Each had its own concentration of shipping lying off-shore and its own naval vessels engaging land targets. This shelling was proceeding in a methodical, almost leisurely manner, denoted each time by deep red flashes from the guns and clouds of ochre smoke. Occasionally a fountain of water showed where a mine had been detonated, or an enemy salvo fallen, but on the whole there seemed to be little opposition from the shore.

On the beaches the tide was ebbing, leaving some of the landing craft high and dry; there were few soldiers and little activity to be seen. This was in such marked contrast to what we had expected that for some time I almost believed that the few craft visible were derelict, and that the assault had been thrown back into the sea. The fact that all the men already ashore had vanished seemed to support this view; the extensive flooding behind the line of the dunes lent it probability; the dull grey cumulus clouds which began to form below us, spreading and joining up with each other until the ships were almost hidden, added the sombre tones of defeat and failure. It was difficult to believe that the Atlantic Wall could have been overthrown so rapidly, with so little sound and fury; on the contrary it seemed more probable that we had been surprised by the flooding of the hinterland and that the enemy, sitting behind the inundations, had broken the assault on the beaches. It was only on landing, after a two-hour patrol, that I was able to re-assure myself.

By mid-day, when we flew out again, the weather had improved and was almost perfect: the sun shone on a placid bay and the sky, except for some scattered cumulus over the land, was cloudless. The destroyer, settled down in shallow water, was surrounded by a sheet of oil; in the east some big fires were burning on and behind the British beaches; the warships were still carrying out some sporadic shelling; otherwise there was no sign of fighting. Landing-craft were plying between ship and shore with as little interference as if they had been Isle of Wight ferries, while on the beaches men and vehicles were forming up; we even saw one little convoy setting off inland along an improvised corduroy track.

At two points there was evidence of Bomber Command's contribution to the assault, at Pointe de la Percée and St Martin de Vanneville. Heavy coastal batteries were located at each place and in them were the guns which Rommel had promised should defeat the invasion before even a foothold had been gained. There seemed to be four to six heavy concrete structures, with an interval of about fifty or hundred yards between each, and these we supposed housed the guns and magazines. In both cases these emplacements formed the centre of an area of complete devastation; this in turn was surrounded by a ring where bomb-craters were scattered, not over-lapping; beyond this again was unscarred country. It was clear that a large force had been employed and the bombing, in its accuracy and concentration, was exemplary.

The central area of devastation, in particular, provided conclusive evidence of the annihilating effect of heavy bombs. All traces of timber and vegetation had vanished as if it had never been. Even in the outer circle, where there was no concentration, the hedges were ragged, indeed hardly recognisable, the trees stripped of branches and foliage like the skeletons of Delville Wood; in the inner zone they were simply not visible. In their place was a wilderness of sandy craters; they were not only overlapping, but in many cases stick after stick of bombs must have fallen successively on the same ground. The earth had been turned over to a considerable depth, and the spoil flung and blown about until it had the appearance of being higher than, and overflowing onto, the surrounding country.

Among these craters we could see the remains of the concrete gun-emplacements and magazines. Examinations after capture showed that the dimensions of each of these structures was approximately 60 feet by 30 feet; the guns were bedded in concrete floors six feet deep; overhead was another six to seven feet of concrete surmounted by earth; the walls were no less than ten feet thick, also of concrete. It was small wonder that Rommel counted on their functioning.

An American scientific observer, examining the ruins of the battery at St Martin de Vanneville, after it had been captured reported as follows:

> ... near-misses to the gun-positions which were under construct-ion smashed much of the re-inforcing and generally disrupted the formwork. Direct hits on the magazine destroyed the entire structure by setting-off the ammunition in one case and destroying the roof over part of the structure in another case. Near misses contributed considerably to the total damage to the magazines by cracking the walls and the roof. Direct hits on the personnel quarters perforated the roofs and completely destroyed the structures. Approximately 90% of the installation was destroyed by the bombing.

In all, on the night of 5th June, no less than 5,300 tons were dropped by Bomber Command on the coastal batteries of Normandy; when the invasion fleets made landfall at dawn next morning only one of these batteries was able to offer serious resistance.

The wing flew its fourth patrol at dusk that evening. In the north-west the sun sank from a cloudless sky into the warm, resplendent haze which lay over the sea; in the south-east the rich colours had already drained away and left an almost full moon, pale like parchment and seemingly over-sized, shining against the austere, bluish background.

II

I stood in the briefing-room, a canvas-covered space between two motor-caravans, and watched the rain which, with interruptions, had been falling for two days. The clouds were very low and showed no sign of breaking or lifting; the weather-forecast held out no hope.

Only one patrol had been possible that day. We had taken off in poor visibility and had penetrated a belt of weather near the Isle of Wight, where the clouds had forced us down below the level of the cliff-tops at St Catherine's Point; to the south of this, conditions had improved and we had been able to fly over the bridge-head with an adequate ceiling and visibility. At this time, however, D + 3, there were no landing grounds in Normandy and I had been worried throughout the patrol in case the weather should become impossible at the Sussex bases, a hundred miles behind us. Eight minutes before our normal time, I had received orders to land and had guessed that conditions were probably deteriorating. As we had flown north, the ceiling had gradually become lower and lower, and visibility below it had become progressively worse. I had been relieved to think that, if my navigation was correct, we should strike the coast where it was low-lying: to the north, the clouds would certainly be down on the South Downs – making them invisible and menacing – while to east and west even the cliffs at Beachy and St Catherine's might be shrouded in them. With a squadron in formation behind me, it would have been a fatal mistake if I had even run unsuspectingly into a position from which we could not extricate ourselves. I had visualised the possibilities uneasily: high ground, the top hidden in cloud, suddenly showing ahead through the rain; some pilots seeing it too late and hitting it; others perhaps colliding in their efforts to turn away from it; others trying to climb up through thousands of feet of cloud and possibly losing control; the squadron dispersed; almost certain casualties. To avoid these eventualities I had, as soon as I had seen the coast, begun to turn at once and had made a full orbit while taking stock of the position; I had been unable to recognize the place, but it was without doubt the Sussex coast. Visibility was less than a mile, so it was impossible to tell whether conditions over land were better or worse than over the sea. I had crossed the coast – it had to be done sooner or later – and had found with considerable relief that the cloud-base was just high enough above the trees and houses to enable us to maintain formation and manoeuvre. Fifteen minutes later we had all been safely on the ground.

Now, in the briefing-room the two Norwegian squadron commanders and I were trying to decide whether or not we should fly a dusk-patrol that evening. Mine had been the only squadron to operate at tea-time, and Christie and Lundsten wanted to hear what the conditions had been. I described them.

'I think we ought to go if we possibly can,' said Christie. They both spoke excellent English, as did all the Norwegian pilots.

'The point is, the weather on the other side is quite good; if none of us takes off, they then might be able to stage a pretty big attack. Besides, we might have some fun!'

'I think,' said Lundsten, 'that if they had been capable of making a big attack they would have made it yesterday.' He was referring to the fact that bad weather had then reduced the fighter cover over the bridgehead from nine to only three squadrons.

'He may not have been ready. Besides, some squadrons were there and he probably didn't realise that others weren't.'

'I don't know about that,' said Lundsten. 'It was pretty obvious: the Controller kept calling them up without getting an answer.'

'Yes, that's true, but look what happened afterwards: as soon as they told us to go home the bastards came out and did some bombing.' Christie was nothing if not offensively-minded.

'I think you must look at it like this,' I put in. 'We can't guess whether he will attack or not, but we know that he has had time to concentrate his aircraft, and he obviously can't afford to wait indefinitely. If I were in his place, I'd wait for an opportunity like this: fine in France, clampers in England. It's a chance in a hundred. The Hun is partial to dusk, and he believes in massive blows, so if he has any sort of clue, I think he'll turn on the heat to-night.'

I still believed that the Germans would make a last attempt to dispute our mastery of the air, and that a great air battle was therefore imminent. It seemed inevitable. Germany's last chance of winning the war lay in repelling the invasion: if she achieved that, she was entitled to entertain some hopes of a compromise peace. But not otherwise. Moreover the prestige of Hitler and the Party leaders was bound up with the campaign in the west. For months the German papers had been harping on the strength of the Atlantic Wall; the Führer himself, by publicly inviting the Allies to attempt the invasion, had staked his reputation on it. Now that it had failed him, it seemed as if the time for desperate measures had arrived. The Luftwaffe and the U-boats had both been under careful conservation for some time, apparently to meet just such a situation as this. Losses might be heavy, but life had never counted for much in the Third Reich when assessed against a vital objective. Pilots of all sorts were being trained, it was known, to fly single-engine fighters; the production of these aircraft was reputedly 1,100 a month; recent losses had been light. It was therefore reasonable to suppose that the Germans possessed a large reserve of fighters; these they might employ to enable them to achieve and use air superiority just long enough for their submarines, bombers, torpedo-aircraft and fighter bombers to jeopardize our whole position in France.

Christie and I were both in favour of taking off, even if conditions made it hazardous to do so. Lundsten, however, did not seem to be altogether converted to our beliefs and, though he was at pains to hide it, was obviously loth to risk his squadron in such weather. His eyes, as he agreed with us that the dusk patrol should be done, were noticeably troubled. He seemed in fact, to be full of foreboding. Since then I have often thought of this meeting, and of the decision we then took, and wondered whether Lundsten, who did not habitually take the part of caution, had received premonition of what awaited him.

The Controller decided that the weather was too uncertain for more than two squadrons to operate; since we had flown last, the

Spitfires from 132 wing providing fighter cover to the ground forces in France.

Pilots of the Royal Norwegian Air Force in 132 Wing on a landing strip in France.

task fell to the Norwegians. Christie and I were wrong: no German attack took place that evening. And Lundsten, who had been right, was by a tragic error shot down by Allied anti-aircraft fire and killed.

*

For the next three weeks we did little but patrol over the bridgehead and shipping. Looking back, it is difficult to distinguish one flight from another: only certain scenes stand out clearly in memory, unrelated to the sequence of which they form a part. Sometimes, when the tide was full, the beaches looked as lively as anthills; there were others, at the ebb, when landing-craft lay high on the sand, and nothing seemed to stir below. On some days, under cloudless skies, convoys would come steaming into the bay, the merchantmen symmetrically spaced in two lines, and begin to discharge almost at once; on others, when the famous north-easter was blowing, the pitching ships lay to, their anchors undischarged and the seas broke over the deserted piers and breakwaters.

Sometimes the evenings were cloudless and the sun, sinking into banks of amethyst haze, threw a golden path towards us across the water so that we could see the tiny corrugations of the waves sharply and precisely engraved. Sometimes below motionless pearl-grey cloud, the Isle of Wight and Anvil Point, delineated in exact silhouette, were visible from beyond Cherbourg across miles of sea on which not even a catspaw broke the flawless surface.

There were mornings when the cumulus clouds had formed in such profusion that the whole world below them seemed to be in blue shadow, and they themselves, with their tops radiant in sunlight, had the appearance of great icebergs half-submerged in a magical ultra-marine sea. There were afternoons when great rainstorms drove across the Seine Bay, making segments of it invisible and, to us flying low over the white-horses, seeming to change its whole shape and character. During a long strenuous month the squadron flew more than 1250 hours.

During this time the front was gradually established and extended. Within a week of the first landing, the Americans had thrust south-west from Bayeux to capture the Forêt de Cerisy;

The author gets some assistance.

within a fortnight they had put a noose round the neck of the
Cotentin Peninsula; before the end of the month they had delivered
Cherbourg to the Allies.

As time passed without any air-fighting, we began to envy the
Typhoons their role of supporting the troops on the ground. We
used to watch them take off, blowing up immense clouds of dust,
from the strips which had just been constructed among the
cornfields of Calvados, climb behind our lines to 8,000 feet, fly
southward to the lines, dive on their target, eight aircraft in
succession, and zoom back towards friendly territory to reform for
another attack. Each time the enemy reacted with an angry barrage
of light flak. The Typhoons looked like children playing an exciting
game with a malignant but partly disabled animal. It was no game,
however, that they played. By 23rd June I heard that two of the three
wing commanders whom I had known, and four of the eight
squadron commanders, had been killed or were missing. We were to
have an opportunity later of inspecting their retribution to the
enemy for these grievous losses.

Long before the end of June it had become clear that the enemy did not intend to dispute our mastery of the air over the bridgehead in Normandy. The number of patrols flown by each squadron had been reduced from four each day to two. Interest revived momentarily when one of the Norwegian squadrons one day encountered a number of enemy fighters and shot down four of them without loss, but on the whole the Luftwaffe remained conspicuously absent. At the end of June we heard that the wing was to cease carrying out patrols and was to resume fighter-sweeps and escorts. None of us was sorry.

*

On 13th June the first flying-bombs were launched against this country. At dawn on the 18th, rushing out of my tent in the half-light of dawn, with the grass wet underfoot and heavy with pollen, I had been in time to see one fly over the aerodrome. On the 19th I took off with Brown, one of four Australians in the squadron, and flew eastward to Beachy Head to try to intercept any that were sent over. It was a perfect evening in mid-summer: the north-west was aglow with the splendours of a solemnly sinking sun. We climbed through a warm haze to the colder air above and watched the circumference of heaven change from purple to amethyst and, as the light drained away, from amethyst to blue. There was no wind; the sea was unruffled; on land what little smoke there was – for it was already late for householders – rose placidly upwards. It was a scene of immaculate peace.

As we passed over Brighton and Newhaven we heard reports of a flying bomb near Beachy, but we arrived too late to intercept it. There followed a lull in activity, during which we patrolled at 5,000 feet off the headland, while the light gradually faded. At last the Controller called to say that he had a customer for us, twenty-five miles away, heading for Beachy; we dropped our long-range tanks and increased speed and vigilance. A minute or two later I spotted a pinpoint of light to the south-west and, finding that it was moving, turned to head it off. As we closed with it, pinpoints of light, like electric sparks, appeared behind it. At first I imagined that this was some phenomenon of its fiery wake, but soon guessed that an invisible fighter had forestalled us and was attacking it. As we watched the light went out; there was an interval of perhaps ten or fifteen seconds before the explosion followed. The bomb had fallen near the shore, west of Bexhill.

Brown and I resumed patrol at Beachy. At last, at a quarter past eleven, the Controller warned us of another customer. It was Brown who first saw it in a position slightly west of where we had spotted the other. We dived down on its port beam, using full power. As I began to swing in behind it, I noticed that there were four aircraft behind it, barely discernible because it was by now almost dark, and that the first of these was shooting. I pulled up above him to avoid his fire and as I did so saw him break away; judging the others to be out of range, I slipped into his place, hoping that they would have the sense to hold their fire.

The target now appeared as a light in front of me; it was impossible to see anything of its structure or do more than guess its range. I steadied my aircraft and waited until I was exactly in line astern; then, using both hands on the sticks, and aiming slightly high, I fired a two-second burst. Flashes round the light showed that hits had been scored. I fired again and the result was startling: the light suddenly expanded until it had become an immense sheet of flame which seemed to fill the whole sky in front of me. I pulled back desperately on the stick and felt the aircraft rise as it tried to clear the immense, glowing obstacle. It almost did so, but as the core of the explosion passed beneath me it seemed as if the aircraft flew through the flames at the circumference. My first thought was for the fabric on my control-surfaces; I was relieved to find that handling was apparently normal. My next concern was for my engine, but it was running normally and all the instruments were steady. I noticed that I had caught the pilotless aircraft just before it had crossed the coast at Eastbourne. After a short delay Brown and I joined up again and, flying back together, landed on a flare path at about midnight, as the last glow in the north-west was extinguished by the deepening night.

III

15th June 1944 I awoke to find that it was still quite dark. My tent-flaps were open at both ends, and the night air felt sweet and pure; a faint breeze was stirring the foliage of the trees beside which our tents were pitched and the stars, I could see, were shining placidly.

Outside someone was moving about with a torch. Warm and comfortable in my sleeping-bag, I lay still, hoping against hope that we were not being called for an early-morning operation. The war was distant and uninviting; more than that, it was folly, dangerous to those who took part in it. Why should one pretend that one enjoyed killing and risking being killed? It was at times like these that one saw life and all its pursuits in their true light. In the evening one might feel differently; one argued with one's friends and drank a little beer and then one believed that there was nothing finer to bring some of one's fellow human-beings to an early, violent death; and by that time one had become such a fine fellow that one did not entertain the possibility that, as one did, so might one be done by. At such times life was simple, and one had no need to question it or to look below its surface. Yet that was the illusion; this – the faint scent of hay, the early stirrings of the world, a sense of well-being and universal benevolence, a longing for comfort and security – this was the reality. The arguments had passed through my mind so often that I could add nothing new to them; I only wished again that I had been born more naturally aggressive.

The figure with the torch came towards my tent, slipped inside and began to shake me gently by the shoulder. 'There's a show at first light, sir; breakfast is laid on for four-thirty and briefing at five.' It was the pilot who had been on duty at the telephone during the night. I pretended to be waking up.

'Good show. Any idea where we're going?'

'It's a sweep, I think, and we're to land in the bridgehead; haven't heard any details yet.'

'Right. You've woken the others, of course?'

At five-thirty the wing took off and set course for France with the wing commander, leading one of the Norwegian squadrons in the centre, my squadron stepped up 1,000 feet to starboard, and the other Norwegian squadron stepped up 2,000 feet to port. We crossed the French coast near Dieppe at 10-12,000 feet and bore on south-east for Beauvais. The sun had just risen into a cloudless sky; below us France lay half-swathed in a thin mist which clung close to the ground, so that the tree-tops protruded through it. The sun was not high enough to light the colours of the countryside, which still looked blue, as does a range of distant hills.

At Beauvais we made a slow turn to starboard, in the course of which we swung across the formation to the port side, changing places with the second Norwegian squadron, and with the sun at our backs set course for the Seine and Evreux. As we crossed the river we could see broken bridges above and below Vernon. At Evreux the wing commander called to say that he would make one orbit of the aerodrome; almost at once another voice reported aircraft below and, as he did so, I saw several sections half-roll and lose themselves to view in long dives.

Looking down I noticed a number of Fw190s, well below us, painted in grey-green camouflage, unmistakable although their black-crosses were too small to distinguish. As I circled above a Spitfire, flying much faster, began closing in on one of them. I watched fascinated, as a man might watch a body in a guillotine when the knife is hoisted. There was no time to experience hope that he might escape, nor fear lest he did, and I only felt certain that if he did not move he was a dead man. Flashes at the Spitfire's gun-ports and a tenuous stream of grey smoke behind the cannons denoted that the attack had begun. The range was short now; still the 190 did not attempt to evade.

Suddenly bright flashes broke out, almost simultaneously, in different parts of his wings and fuselages. As the first Spitfire broke away a second one opened fire. The 190 seemed to falter, almost to stagger, pulled up slightly hesitating, then turned onto its back and dived into the ground. It had been less than twenty seconds since our aircraft had first dived from six or eight thousand feet above; probably the German pilot did not know, perhaps never knew, that they were behind him. The aircraft fell in the garden of a house situated on the outskirts of a village; on impact it exploded in a leaping, dull-red flame and, with black petrol-smoke billowing up from it, continued for some time to burn on the ground. Almost immediately afterwards a second explosion to the south showed that another aircraft had crashed.

At this point an Me109 came into view below us, flying outside the general area of the dog-fight, and the section which I was leading dived onto it. Our speed, which had built up in the dive to about 400 mph was much greater than his and in consequence we found ourselves over-shooting. Waterhouse, in front of me, was able to fire a short burst, but I was compelled to break off my attack. He had clearly seen us diving on him and, by turning in towards and under us, had taken the correct evasion. I zoom-climbed until reduced speed had made my controls more easy to handle, and then dropped a wing to see what had become of the 109. The country below was partly wooded, and at first I could not pick him out against this drab background, but at last I saw him, a small object momentarily outlined against a swathe of mist, a couple of thousand feet almost directly below me; the other member of my section had vanished. I dived again to attack and again, at precisely the right moment, he suddenly whipped into a tight left-handed turn towards me. It was clear that this was no inexperienced pilot. My speed was still considerably greater than his and I was fast closing in on him; at about 600 yards, with his aircraft 30° off my line of flight, I opened fire. He appeared to tighten his turn and, with my superior speed making negative my superior manoeuvrability, I found it difficult to keep my lead ahead of him.

Seeing no results from my first burst, I increased the deflection until he was out of sight below the nose of my aircraft – the range had now decreased to 300 yards – and fired again. I was still diving at full power, and the speed and the rate of turn were so great that my vision was becoming grey and misty. I was in fact on the threshold of a black-out. In this condition I judged it unwise to try to follow the enemy aircraft where he was flying above the tree-tops; misjudgment of altitude would have been too easy. There was the added danger, at that height of fouling his slipstream and momentarily losing control. I therefore relaxed my rate of turn and, flying off at a tangent, slid behind him at a distance of not more than 100 yards.

Gaining height again, I looked down and saw what appeared to be white smoke pouring from him in profusion, so at once assumed that I had hit his cooling-system. The effect was exactly similar to a severe glycol leak. I found, however, that I was congratulating myself too soon, for the smoke ceased abruptly and, looking back, I saw that it had been caused by condensation as he flew through a wisp of mist.

From above, I could see that he was still flying at tree-top level and still turning to the left; the significance of this move did not strike me, until afterwards. For the third time I dived on him and for the third time he waited until I was about 800 yards distant and then turned violently towards me. As soon as he did this, streamers of white vapour flew back from his wing-tips, so that he appeared to be cleaving the air, as indeed he was, for very life. This time I pulled my sight right through him and held my fire until he was invisible under my engine; only one of the two cannon responded. Again I found, as I closed in on him, that his inferior speed was enabling him to turn inside me, and again I was forced to slide behind him. This time, on looking round, I found that the air was full of the white puffs of light flak, and I realised that he had completed a full circle so as to lead me back over this defended area. So absorbed had I been before that I had not noticed the flak.

As so often happens in air warfare, from being the hunter I had suddenly become the hunted. With only one cannon firing, separated from my squadron, far behind the enemy lines, exposed to intense light flak, it would have been stupidity or stubbornness to have persevered; it was not without remorse, nevertheless, that I left my quarry and the danger area. Though I did not know it at the time, my aircraft had already been hit and my radiator very nearly punctured.

During this brief engagement, which cannot have lasted more than two minutes, I had been in the state of excitement and absorption, almost obliviousness, which is usual in air fighting. As I climbed back into the bright sky the excitement died and I had leisure to consider my position. My pursuit had separated me not only from my section but from the rest of the wing; there was no other aircraft in sight. The combats appeared to be over, for section-leaders were busy on the R/T gathering their flocks. Their voices, loud and familiar were re-assuring, but I wished heartily that I could see some of them. I had sacrificed all my advantage of height and was now fifty miles behind the enemy lines, alone under a cloudless sky in which a menacing sun was shining. Even the 109 could not be altogether disregarded; he was still flying ventre à terre when last seen, but appeared to be undamaged, and might conceivably shadow me and attack from below when my vigilance was relaxed. Beside the faint apprehension with which I regarded this threat to my rear, was keen disappointment at my failure to destroy him; my chance had come and I had failed to grasp it.

As I climbed up, I could hear one of the Norwegians calling to say that he had been hit; many voices, sounding more concerned than his, offered advice and assistance. Later he was heard to remark, in an even conversational tone, that his engine was failing and that he was about to bale out. I was still in the area in which the combats had taken place and had reached 6-7,000 feet flying fast and irregularly, when I suddenly found myself set upon by four Fw190s. In the mysterious way of aircraft, they appeared as if from nowhere; one moment the sky was empty, the next I was taking desperate evasive measures to keep them from my tail. While doing so I managed to call Venus, give my height and position, and ask for help.

On first sighting them, I had felt that unless help arrived I was bound to be shot down: they were too many, and I was too far from friendly territory, to have any hope of eluding them. A series of thoughts and emotions followed each other rapidly through my head: self-reproach for having thrown away my early tactical advantages and brought myself to this pass; anger towards my section – unjust but entertained in spite of the knowledge that it was unjust – for having lost touch with me; remorse at having exposed myself once too often to danger which I had barely escaped before; dread that I should now never return home, accompanied by a penitent yearning for it; petulance that no one came to help me; and, above all these, a blend of fear and desperation, the sense of being trapped.

During this time I was, whenever my evasive manoeuvres showed it, continuing to climb at maximum power. At first the 190s had had the advantage of speed – they must have dived on me – as well as of numbers; gradually, however, I found that my aircraft was beginning to turn the tables on them. Their attacks were ill-organized and I found, by constant all-round vigilance, and violent evasion at the right moment, that I was able to avoid them. When this duel had lasted perhaps three minutes, and I was beginning to feel the pace, another Spitfire joined me. I learned afterwards that the pilot was Brown. The 190s at once became more wary and less aggressive. I found that I was beginning to out-climb them and noticed one, at which Brown had fired, emitting heavy brown smoke. These two factors must have caused the remainder to dive away for, as suddenly as they had appeared, they vanished.

I throttled back, but continued to fly irregularly to prevent further surprises. Spotting four Spitfires, and having lost Brown to sight, I flew to join them. They proved, however, to be Me109s. By this time I was less apprehensive of mere numbers and was not unduly perturbed. They made pretence of attacking me, but clearly had little heart in it and, as soon as a repetition of my previous tactics began to give me an advantage of height over them, they dived away.

I looked at my altimeter and found that I was at 15,000 feet. With two short intervals, I reckoned that I must have been flying at full throttle for nearly ten minutes; my engines, however, sounded sweet and all the instruments were steady and impassive; I found this astonishing when I was flustered, sweating apprehensive, out of breath, disappointed and relieved. There was nothing to be heard over the R/T, and this gave me the impression that I was alone in the area. I decided to search the whole sky before setting course for the bridge-head; there was nothing to be seen except, four or five thousand feet below, two aircraft flying west in loose formation. I was uncertain what to do: I was admirably placed for an attack from the sun; but I was alone and in making it I should expose my own tail to any enemy similarly placed above me. Moreover, there seemed to be far more enemy aircraft in the area than Spitfires, and only one of my cannons was functioning.

Probably if I had not often regretted missing a similar opportunity two years before I should have played for safety; as it was, pricked on by the chagrin of having allowed the 109 to escape, I decided to accept the risk. I dived on them out of the sun and was quickly able to identify them as Fw 190s; they evidently had not seen me, for they were flying westward, unsuspecting, in a loose echelon. My overtaking speed was not very great and I was able to take deliberate aim at the nearer of the two; at 400 yards range I fired.

After the momentary pause which always elapses while the projectiles are in flight, I saw first one and then a series of strikes on his port wing and fuselage; pieces came away from the main structure and drifted back towards me, followed by smoke dense enough to hide the whole starboard side of his fuselage and wing-root. Next instant a larger object, which might have been the cockpit hood, also flew away.

As I was watching those developments, I suddenly became aware of red tracer flashing past my starboard wing. I had often heard other pilots describe this phenomenon, but had never experienced it before; there was no means of telling how near it was, but it appeared to be an arm's length only from the cockpit. Keyed up as I was, and consciously apprehensive of such an attack in my unprotected rear, I wrenched the aircraft round to port with all the strength conferred by fear, and put it into a juddering climbing-turn. Half-blacked out as I was in this manoeuvre, I could see nothing of the aircraft attacking me, but could only sit wincing, during ten interminable seconds, in the physical and mental dread at hearing those fateful internal reports which tell that an aircraft has received its death-blow. But nothing hit me, and the attacking aircraft must have dived past me as I was turning, for I never saw it. But two or three thousand feet below I glimpsed an open parachute and assumed that the pilot of the 190 which I had attacked had baled out.

I climbed back into the sun at full throttle without relaxing until I had reached 15,000 feet again and had joined forces with two Norwegians. With them I flew north-west to the bridgehead and landed at the Bazenville strip.

It was surprising to find that it was only just after seven o'clock: so much had happened in so short a time that it seemed to be midday at least. The sun, too, was already high and the still air hot. The contrast in conditions was startling; we had come down from the thin pure air of the middle-heavens to the heavy mid-summer atmosphere at ground level. Dust lay thick everywhere, on the grass, in the tall unripened corn, on the hedgerow elms; every blade, ear and leaf was coated with it. Below the wire-mesh of the runway and on the cleaned taxi-tracks it lay in a fine powder, inches deep. Every aircraft that moved on the ground stirred up a small sandstorm which hung in the motionless air until dispersed by time.

I was grateful to step out of the aircraft and stretch my legs; my shirt, I found, was wringing with sweat and I was glad to expose it to the sun. The warmth of this drowsing countryside made me feel sleepy and self-satisfied. As always at times of fruition, life seemed very good.

The pilots, who had dispersed their aircraft about the field, began to assemble in twos and threes, all talking excitedly.

'Sum clot said they were friends, but Ah could see they were Won-nineties. We came in behind one of them and as soon as Cas broke away Ah let him have it. Ah've never known such a stew-pid bastard, he didn't do anything. Ah saw our strikes all over 'm, and he just turned on his back and went straight into the decks.'

George Lonnan always drawled in his broad Lancashire vowels in a high pitch if he wished to emphasize a word. He was one of the oldest members of the squadron, almost the doyen of the sergeant pilots; as such, he enjoyed indulging his idiosyncrasies, always wore many-coloured sweaters and, even during the hottest days of summer, on the ground or in the air, was never without his suede flying-boots and thick woollen socks. Before the war he had been a textile-clerk in Bolton; now he was a fully-licensed character: independent, outspoken, an inveterate grumbler, an incessant talker, in little things idle and crafty as an old sweat, in big ones a model of keenness and determination, impatient of external authorities, but intensely loyal to his squadron and to those who commanded his affection or respect.

'The stew-pid little baastard,' he was saying, 'that'll teach him a smaart lesson to keep his eyes open in future.'

To pretend to be disappointed in the quality of his opponent was a pardonable affectation; as an old hand he felt he must disguise his excitement and pleasure, and this fatherly exhibition of sorrow rather than anger was his method of doing so. Behind the pretence I could see that he was overjoyed at his success, simply and unaffectedly overjoyed without suffering any of the qualms which might have beset a more complicated character. His job was to shoot down enemy aircraft and at last the fates had been kind and he had shot one down; that was a source of great comfort, and he could not stop himself talking about it. But he owed it to his reputation, and to experienced Sergeant-pilots everywhere, to pretend that the fish had been such a small one that it had left him unmoved, that he was even thinking of throwing it back.

Later in the morning we learned that the wing had destroyed eight enemy fighters for the loss of the Norwegian who had said he must bale out; even he was believed to have been hit by flak; not shot down from the air. Of these eight we claimed three without loss.

My aircraft had been hit by light flak in the starboard wing; the splinter had damaged the radiator cowling, missing the vulnerable honeycomb by one foot, and had punctured the starboard tyre. I watched the sweating servicing commandos supporting the wing on their backs while the wheel was changed. And I thought of the Norwegian, probably being hunted in the woods, and of the Germans lying dead in their burnt-out aircraft. What a chancy game it was. One foot at 350 mph, I reflected, represented one five-hundredth of a second.

IV

It was a warm mid-summer afternoon and I was looking forward to passing it lazily in my tent. Venus wanted to lead the squadron and, after a month of the most intensive flying of my career, I was glad to stand down. There was something luxurious in seeing others concerned with the details of briefing, noting down heights of patrol, time and place of rendezvous, role of escorting fighters, while oneself being free of the responsibility. It was pleasant, too, to lie on one's camp-bed, with both flaps of the tent open, and to think that, for at least two and a half hours, until the aircraft had returned and been re-fuelled, one was free to read or sleep or muse, or to do anything one pleased. The sense of relaxation was all the sweeter because it was so short-lived; in three hours' time one would probably be worrying over another operation, but for the moment one was free.

I read and dozed in the meadow overlooking the airfield and then, when the aircraft were due to return, walked the six hundred yards to the squadron dispersal point. The pilots were bringing their parachutes and flying-kit in to the hut, and I did not at once realise that anything unusual had happened.

'Who was it, d'you know?' someone asked.

'Reg Emery, I think, it sounded like his voice.'

'Yes, he was Blue 4.'

It took some time before I could piece the story together. The wing had been patrolling over France in the Dieppe area when Emery had developed engine-trouble; he had fallen so far behind that the leading pair of his section of four had never seen him again, while his No 1, turning back to help him, had lost him to view as he glided northwards at about 18,000 feet over the French coast. He had been given a course to steer for Beachy Head, and had been heard making the correct emergency transmissions but, by an unlucky chance, the receiving station in England had been temporarily unserviceable, so that no fix on his position had been obtained. After a short interval he was heard to say that his motor was dead, that he was about half-way across the Channel, on the point of baling out.

There was some doubt about the spot at which he had crossed the French coast; a port had been half-seen through a gap in the clouds, but some said it was Dieppe, others Le Tréport. It seemed then that Emery was somewhere near the middle of the triangle formed by Beachy Head, Le Tréport and Dieppe. On the map it looked small enough, but I knew how poorly maps represented those endless acres of sea, one indistinguishable from another, and cursed the ill-luck which had robbed us of his exact position. Earlier in the year I had spent many hours sweeping the North Sea in unsuccessful search for lost pilots, and was under no illusions about the difficulties of spotting so minute an object as a dinghy.

As I made my final preparations and briefed the pilots on the height, formation, and method of search, I found myself in an irritable and aggrieved frame of mind. It was useless to tell myself that a pilot was in distress and needed our best assistance; my physical self answered sulkily that it had been promised a quiet afternoon and, though it would do its best, it resented the necessity. This mood persisted until dispersed by the growing interest of the search.

Six of us took off and flew along the Sussex coast past Brighton, where Emery lived I remembered, and Newhaven, to Beachy Head. With two aircraft on one side and three on the other, all in line abreast at 800 yard intervals, I dived over the cliffs and, at 200 feet, flew carefully onto my first course. The weather was almost cloudless and a bright sun heightened the contrast between the blue of the sea and the white of the English cliffs; the wind was 15 mph from the south-west, visibility excellent, sea slight to moderate. Occasionally a white horse broke the surface.

I had decided that it would be unwise to set too much store by Emery's belief that he was in mid-Channel when he was about to bale out; we could not be certain that it was a visual estimate and, if it were not, it was probably unreliable. There were, however, reasonable grounds for supposing him inside the triangle formed by

Beachy Head and the two French ports, but to cover the unforeseen we had determined to search not only the middle of the triangle, but the whole of it to within eight miles of either coast-line.

Flying south on the first leg, it was not long before one of us saw something in the water and circled low over it to investigate; the rest of us, to preserve our formation, were compelled to do likewise. The object proved to be a cask; the action of water on the wood had made it bright yellow in colour so that at even a short distance it was easily confused with the dinghy we were looking for. We set course again. Within two minutes we were circling again in false hopes; this time it was a basket which had caught the eye. The third time it was a marker flag, raised from the sea on the end of a half-submerged pole, which attracted attention.

It seemed probable that a ship had foundered in the area, for the water was full of flotsam; whenever we were in any doubt we felt bound, for fear of missing Emery, to circle and scrutinize such objects. It was comforting to me to know that virtually nothing was escaping us, yet I began to feel faintly uneasy at the delay which each orbit imposed. It seemed possible that we should not, as I had planned, be able to cover the whole area before fuel shortage compelled us to return.

Gradually the French cliffs, which had first appeared as a faint line when we were in mid-Channel, began to reveal their contours. With their northern faces in shadow, they appeared grey and severe, wholly unlike the friendly chalk of Sussex.

I made a mental note of the point at which we had made landfall and then, when I judged that we were eight miles offshore, I gave the order to turn-about to port. These turns, it had been arranged beforehand, should be wide enough to send the most westerly aircraft home along the out-coming track of the most easterly one. In this way we hoped to cover the ground methodically, after the manner of a man mowing a lawn; yet the system was at the mercy of our judgement, for the sea, unlike a lawn, showed no marks of our passing.

Heading north we again passed through the area of flotsam, and were again delayed in fruitless examination of wreckage. Soon afterwards I was able, with relief, to give the order to change fuel-feed from auxiliary to main tanks; I had been worried in case anything should occur to distract my attention and make me forget the order, for at that height, with no room to bale out and no time for the engine to recover, it was almost certain death to allow a motor to cut through fuel-starvation.

Eight miles south of Beachy we turned about again and set a slightly divergent course to the first one. In mid-Channel we saw a motor-launch which was clearly helping in the search but had apparently seen no more than we. Off the French coast I again noticed the cliffs; as far as I could judge we had made about the correct easting. Northward-bound once more we saw two low-flying aircraft, which proved to be a section from an air-sea-rescue squadron engaged upon the same search.

So we flew on, north and south, north and south, gradually moving our patrol eastward. The weather was still perfect. What a magnificent day it would have been, I thought, for sailing. Aircraft were at best exacting and uncomfortable machines: one could never relax and enjoy oneself whole-heartedly in them; there was always some anxiety tugging at one's mind. Was the engine running quite smoothly? Perhaps one ought to open it up to clean the plugs. How much fuel was left? One looked at the gauge again. How much would one need to return to base? One made the calculation again. Was the oil pressure and temperature steady? Another routine glance at the instruments.

An hour had passed in intensive searching. For better vision I was flying with my hood open, and the draughts in the cockpit, together with the strain of constant vigilance, were beginning to make my eyes ache. I wondered whether it was worth continuing much longer; fatigue would soon be reducing our efficiency. We saw a derelict ship's boat and paused to make two or three runs over it, thinking we saw a figure slumped over the thwarts, but it proved to be a bundle of some sort. This was further discouragement: I was by now feeling stiff, uncomfortable, and somewhat daunted. To the north-west Beachy came up over the horizon again. We had already exceeded our planned time, but had still not covered the eastern part of our triangle opposite Le Tréport; I judged that we had enough fuel for one further sweep and decided to make it.

Flying south we saw nothing, but off the French coast, I noticed that we were further east than we should have been; in front of us the cliffs sloped down to the dunes which bordered the Somme estuary to our left. Le Tréport, which should have lain ahead of us, was slightly to the right. To make good the small area which we must therefore have left uncovered, I ordered the turn-about to be made to starboard, instead of to port as hitherto, and we wheeled slowly about for the last big northward. We flew on for some minutes; behind us the French coast sank again below the horizon, some gulls which had been riding on the surface, got up at our approach and dispersed as we passed through them.

I was thinking of nothing, certainly not of Emery, yet apparently still concentrating automatically on the search, when I suddenly became aware that I had seen, just above the horizon in the east, outlined against the darker blue of the sky, a blue-grey loop of smoke. I knew at once what it was, and at once forgot my fatigue and sore eyes in the elation of this almost-abandoned success. That tenuous wisp of smoke had been left hanging in the sky by the last of Emery's distress-rockets.

Before long we had located him and summoned help; our fuel just enabled us to stay until a Walrus landed beside him. Next day he was in the mess again, telling how a succession of aircraft of all types, returning from France, had flown over him; of the rockets he had wasted in trying to attract their attention; of others which had failed to ignite; of being unable to keep himself dry; of growing discomfort and a spreading cold; of sea-sickness and a general wretchedness; of watching us pass, on our last leg southward, a couple of miles to the east of him; of seeing us return northward on a course which would take us a couple of miles to the west of him; of his trepidation in firing his last shot, and the suspense while he waited to see if it would catch our eye.

He told the story simply, without embellishments or retrospective exuberance, so that it was difficult to judge whether he had been shaken by the experience or not. I, however, did not hear it until later for, next day, I began 48 hours' leave.

*

After the discomfort of hotels in war-time, and of travelling, I found that I was relieved to be back in my tent. There was something comforting in the familiar objects in it: the rough fibre-matting on the floor, the tin box which contained my possessions; the deal table with a blanket spread over it for cloth; the green camp-bed, the khaki sleeping-bag, the treasured blue eiderdown; the book I was reading. It was not just that they were mine, and that I was used to them, and liked to have them about me, but that they had a deeper significance which I was dimly able to discern.

Looking back on the Drink combats, I remembered how I had begun the day and how I ended it. In the morning I had woken up in a questioning and unambitious mood, craving comfort and security, reluctant for danger and responsibility; at night, fighting the battles again over a pint of beer, I had felt confident, reckless and enterprising, disinclined to scrutinize values because in accepting them I was, for the moment, happy and successful.

In calmer retrospect it was not difficult to see the falsity of both these moods. The spirit was the prisoner and slave of the flesh. Waking up in warmth and security, with a mind and purpose unfortified for the ordeal of the day, I had shied away at once from the prospect of danger and responsibility; in the evening, when the danger and the responsibility had been successfully faced, and further hazards seemed remote, mental relief and bodily well-being had induced a condition of spontaneous happiness which was little disposed to delve below the surface, lest by so doing it might turn triumph to dust. The one was the product of physical apprehension, the other reaction from it coloured by success; both, it was easy to see, were impostors.

In what bondage the spirit was held by the flesh! Apprehensive in the morning, it had said: 'You are warm and comfortable, above all you are alive, why go on risking your neck; besides ambition is an unworthy thing, especially an ambition which aims no higher than the slaughter of your fellow creatures.' Self-satisfied in the evening, it had changed its tune: 'You are a fine fellow, better than the other man, and there is nothing to be afraid of; why pause to ask if this success is worth anything, when you might forfeit your happiness by finding that it isn't; sit back and enjoy it.' The essential falsity of both these moods was not difficult to detect.

Now I had returned from 48 hours' leave unsettled, as always, and spiritually perplexed. There was something in the life of a squadron which protected individuals from their own inner uncertainties and questionings; that, probably, accounted for my relief on regaining the atmosphere of my tent. Here were symbols of a life of simplicity and singleness of purpose. Remove the individual from this environment, and you exposed him to the insidious blandishments of a more complicated, comfortable and sane way of living.

The impact of this other world on me had had a profoundly disturbing influence. The companionship and devotion of a woman had combined with the chance viewing of two sufficiently ordinary sights – children playing in the sand and a late fisherman sailing his scow up-estuary on a sparkling flood – to bring me to the realization of how much of life was passing me by. This, surely, was the manner in which we were intended to live. What sort of a world was it in which we trained all our faculties for no better object than slaughtering others while preserving ourselves? What values were they which counted a man able or inept according to his abilities in this unhallowed work? Why should we assume it virtue to drive and discipline ourselves for such unworthy objectives? Was it any less logically ludicrous for us to take pride in our human endeavours, directed to base ends, than if the Gadarene swine had gloried in their stamina and speed?

I remembered all the literature of the last war that I had read. What a disillusioned generation that had been! Reactions had varied from bewilderment to the most bitter cynicism: some had suffered the loss of their faith, others were appalled by the horrors of those muddy battlefields; all alike were obsessed with the contrast between the waste and futility of war as it is and the glitter and majesty which men like to attribute to it. Perhaps they had been right. Why should men live in the constant dread of a violent and terrible death? Glory was a chimera, duty only an obligation so long as its ends were wholesome. Beauty was the touchstone: war in all its aspects was unlovely and therefore wrong; the ways of peace were lovely and therefore right.

In this frame of mind I had cast critical glances on my life in the squadron. How studiously we refused to face reality, trying to reduce its complexities to the terms of a game! Our philosophy was one of black and white; we were white, the enemy black, we must take him before he took us. Life was allowed no further standards or significance. The man who fought best was the best man; the man who did not want to fight, or at least did not pretend that he wanted to fight, was a dangerous pariah who must be driven out of the packs. And the object of this game? Perhaps to restore the position as it had been before black was presumptuous enough to challenge white. And what was that position? A jungle of a world in which men and nations prided themselves on, and cultivated, not humility, or toleration, or loving-kindness, but physical courage, might and self-aggrandizement.

I had read and heard these arguments before, a hundred times. Now, when a glimpse into a sane world had thrown me into such perplexity, I found one part of me busy respecting them. The deceptions which the mind practised upon itself in the names of fears and success had not been difficult to detect and scotch; these pleadings, however, while they did not altogether convert me, were specious, and I could not at once put my finger upon this fallacy.

I thought again of the life which a squadron leads. It was exacting, absorbing, almost monastic; it had to be entered whole-heartedly if it was to be entered at all. The manner of living was pre-determined, traditions had to be observed, ideals to be accepted, appearances maintained; the individual could only abide by his charter, seek and confer companionship; give and receive loyalty.

I thought of the unwritten laws of this curious community. Why, for instance, was it a rule that the enemy must never be paid the compliment of being either hated or feared? A tolerant contempt, which might occasionally relax into admiration for an individual or an achievement, was the correct address. Opportunities of meeting him had not only to be sought as a duty but welcomed as a pleasure; the outcome of such a meeting might be made the subject of self-deprecating humour only because it was well-known to be beyond doubt or dispute. No one must pretend that he was not frightened, but no one might behave as if he was. One had never to admit that he was looking forward to completing his tour, or allow an opportunity of prolonging it to pass. Pretentiousness had to be avoided at all costs, and it was incumbent on everyone to indulge in a vein of ironic humour and, without prejudice, pretend that he was a

The author when living under canvas.

poor pilot, an execrable shot, physically a dignified ruin – 'I joined
the RAF, old boy, because it is the only service in which you can do
your fighting sitting down!' – and nervously on the point of a
collapse. Narrow escapes, by the same token, had to be treated by
the escaping pilot as occasions for self-derogatory pleasantry. Death
itself, except when some recent loss made any humour out of place,
had to be brought, as the Dread Reaper, into familiarity and
contempt.

It was easy to dismiss these affectations as puerile, the emanations
of youthful high-spirits, but I was disposed to read more meaning
into them. To begin with, it was impossible to deny that they were
not affectations. No one really believed that the enemy could be
treated with disdain; everyone on the contrary knew that it was
foolish to under-rate him. No one really supposed that friendly
fighters invariably defeated enemy ones; it was well known that they
did not. No one really thought that a pilot derived genuine
amusement from a narrow escape; it was common knowledge that
such events might leave a permanent mark upon his keenness or
daring. No one really could contemplate Death as he would a

buffoon; the appalling shapes which it could take were only too frequently witnessed.

So thinking, I began to see the meaning of the usages which I had regarded as affectations. They formed the psychological armour which we were only too glad to put on to preserve us from the fears and doubts which might otherwise overwhelm us. As individuals we did not believe in these myths, but as members of a squadron we were glad to accept them unquestioningly. That for us was the great beauty of squadron life: it exemplified all our problems for us; that was why, in my perplexity, I had found comfort in the furnishings of my tent, for these were the symbols of that simple life. For us, who had to risk everything for them, the issues had to be well-defined, philosophy to be in black and white. Fear of death or mutilation drove us to our affectations; unwilling to face the dire possibilities, we sought to escape from them in humour and in a formal bluff, and these, while consciously disbelieved, brought comfort.

The impossibility of accepting the hazards of such a life, furthermore, with minds in any way tinged or weakened by doubts, led us to ignore altogether the larger considerations which determined the whole colour and texture of our lives. Individually we should have admitted that man had a higher destiny than schooling himself in exterminating his fellows; as a community we instinctively closed our minds to the possibility. Such thoughts would undermine the very motives which we needed to fulfil our tasks; nor could we afford to have our ethics called in question, least of all by ourselves, if we were to retain the strength and fortitude to carry through our enterprises. This was our armour, and it was only by virtue of it that we were able, day after day, to throw our lives as stakes upon the table.

It was, I felt, almost pathetic, that the spirit, in its struggle with forces almost too strong for us, should be driven to these self-deceptions. No doubt, in our world of make-believe, we were doing violence to the reality and complexity of life; no doubt we were ignoring its beauties, closing our eyes deliberately to its mysteries and meaning, reducing its values to those of a schoolboy's game. Yet to have shied away from the task, and justified our action in the name of beauty, truth, humanity or anything else that suggested itself, would have been the easier, not the harder, task. I remembered again the literature of the last war. How desperately they sought moral justification for actions dictated by physical revolt from the horror, waste and danger of the battlefields. Any man with a bellyful of it can think of a dozen reasons why war should no longer be supported. I recalled my own experiences when wounded. Philosophy maintained that mind and matter could not influence one another, yet here was the flesh colouring the thought of the spirit, influencing its judgment, setting up its values. This was a matter of intellectual honesty: the question was not whether war was evil, but whether war was less or more evil than the forces which we had pledged ourselves to fight. If we believed that these forces were more evil than war, then we did right to drive ourselves on to the struggle. The injury which our self-discipline necessarily did to the depth and fulness of an ideal life were unimportant in the face of our realization and acceptance of a larger truth. Our lives might be maimed and stunted, but they were not fraudulent. Such virtue as we had, I suddenly realised, lay in a simplicity of mind which had been able, where more complicated or developed talents might have failed, in reaching the simple core of a complex problem.

V

The threat of the flying-bombs was so seriously regarded that, towards the end of June, the British and American strategic bomber forces were thrown into the attack on the launching bases. As a result of this decision, we found that our period of patrols was over, and a new phase of escort duties opened for us.

On 2nd July, therefore, we took off in the afternoon and, climbing to 18,000 feet, flew out to a target between St Pol and Douthens which we had been detailed to cover while bombers dealt with it. Over the sea there was no cloud, but France, as was usual at that time of day, was 5/10th covered by fair-weather cumulus. It was against one of these clouds that we first spotted the advancing bomber-stream while yet so far away that it was hardly more distinct than a faint discolouration on a radiant surface, resolving itself only to straining eyes as an agglomeration of tiny specks. A minute later these specks had grown until each was clearly visible; the mass now had the appearance of a swarm of insects. Another minute and they could be identified as aircraft; another, and we could see that they were Lancasters.

On they came, heading south-east in a slight starboard turn. The leading aircraft had formed themselves into a phalanx four or five abreast but the others behind them, though well concentrated, flew in a stream without pretence to formation. To any observer on the ground, uncertain of their destination, the sight must have been terrifying in the extreme. There were one hundred of them and they probably carried six hundred tons of bombs, enough to devastate a small market-town at a single blow.

Watching them from the air I had normally felt impressed by the purposeful and menacing method of their approach. Their black outlines, their hidden but obviously planned intentions, their unswerving descent on their unknown destination, their preoccupation with their task, combined to give them an appearance which had never struck me as anything but formidable. Yet that day it was otherwise. Possibly it was the brightness of the sun, perhaps the remoteness of enemy fighters; whatever the cause, that afternoon they struck me, not as menacing, but only as faintly comic. Usually they reminded me of a commando of driver-ants, implacable and ruthless; now, as they came on in their gentle starboard turn, the phalanx still leading, the others stretched untidily behind, they reminded me irresistibly of the competitors in a French indoor bicycle-race, one of those races which has no beginning and no end, in which no one ever presumes to change the apparently pre-ordained pace and sequence.

When they had bombed, and were beginning to vanish up the back-straight, we too set course for base. As we crossed the French coast at the Somme estuary the Controller called us to tell us to land at Lympne until weather conditions at our own base had improved. This we did and, leaving our aircraft to be re-fuelled, were driven down to the mess for tea. The house we found to be a fine one, built on the brow of the escarpment which looks over Romney Marsh; the garden, though neglected, had clearly been planned with discrimination.

After tea I insisted that Venus should walk round the grounds with me. We had argued before on the merits of the English and American ways of life and I took the theme up again.

'You must admit, Venus, looking round you, that there is something to be said for believing in tradition, slow-growth, maturity, whatever you like to call it.'

'I disagree,' he said, though I could see he was not serious. 'That house, for instance, built in red brick: it's much too big for red-brick, it should be made of steel and concrete.'

I feigned horror. 'Steel and concrete in a garden and climate like this? Steady, Venus. I grant you the brick is still immature, but give it another fifty years and it will have mellowed.'

'Fifty years! You English are always thinking of tradition, the past and the future, never the present. That's typical.'

I took him by the arm and pointed across the Marsh to a Martello-tower on the foreshore. 'You know, Venus, it's lucky you weren't among us a hundred and fifty years ago when those things were built. Tradition really did count for something in those days. Besides, we were an eccentric race then: to nine men out of ten a foreigner wasn't a foreigner but a damned foreigner.'

'And what's the proportion now?'

I laughed. 'I wouldn't like to say. We've grown up, or the virtue has gone out of us: I don't know which. We think you're quite good types now.'

He was by nature impassive and unemotional and it was difficult to guess his real thoughts. At last he said: 'It is lovely, but in Norway we don't think anyone should be rich enough to own a house and a garden like this, while others are poor. There is another side to this picture, you know.'

'You mean too many big towns and too many poor people in them? I agree with you there.'

'Why don't you send more people to your Dominions?'

'Before the war there were two reasons: they wouldn't go, and the Dominions wouldn't have them.'

'Well, you'll have to do something about it if you want your Empire to count for anything after this war.'

That evening, after we had returned to our own base, we went together to a party given by the Czechs at a neighbouring airfield. Venus to me had always seemed a typical product of his race and climate: precise, efficient, purposeful, unsentimental, untroubled by doubts. That night I discovered a trait less practical but perhaps more lovable: he had, since the age of ten, been a passionate follower of English League Football. To me Hapgood, Matthews and Alex James were but names; to him they had been heroes.

*

On 7th July Bomber Command made its first major intervention in the battle of Normandy; to support it, we took off at dusk and flew south towards the bridgehead. Before starting our own engines we had heard the drone of the first bombers passing overhead, but had been prevented by cloud from catching a glimpse of them. Splitting up into sections of four, after setting course, we had climbed through first one then another layer of cloud, each two or three thousand feet thick, to emerge in late sunshine above an ermine carpet. Looking up, we could distinguish the dark, purposeful shapes of the hundreds of Lancasters and Halifaxes for which we were to provide cover. Although still climbing, we gradually overhauled this long procession, for the bombers were heavy-laden and flying slowly. I wondered if the German soldiers in the Caen area had any inkling of what was moving towards them: 2,300 tons of explosives to be delivered in a matter of minutes.

As we approached the Seine Bay the clouds below us cleared and uncovered the Norman coast; the Orne and the adjacent ship-canal stood out clearly in the fading light, pointing like markers at the target. To the south the clouds were piled up in many layers, so that it seemed almost as if an arena had been cleared round the city of Caen. The sun, low in the west, threw a lurid light horizontally across the scene, awakening rich colours on the cloud surfaces, but seeming to throw into darker shadow the sea and earth below.

Arriving on our patrol line west of Caen at 12,000 feet, shortly before the bombers, we were able to watch the first target-indicators fall in cascades of brilliant light, and lie burning on the ground north of the town; the enemy at once re-acted by putting into action the whole of his notoriously heavy flak defences in that sector. As the light drained away with the disappearance of the sun, so the duel which was being fought between the ground defences and the dark invaders became increasingly spectacular. Bombs were bursting in sticks across the target with regular, concussive explosions, one dull-red glow lighting up as its predecessor dived away; smoke and dust were beginning to rise and swirl over the area, sometimes obscuring a group of markers; fires were taking hold; at intervals a fresh cascade of red lights showed where pathfinders were busy renewing target indicators; in the air, prickly flashes came from bursts of heavy flak, while a score of converging, diverging and parallel streams of many-coloured tracer flowed upwards, in a picturesque and leisurely way, from the lighter guns.

It was soon too dark to distinguish the bombers against the darker background of the land and, before long, it was becoming difficult, even at our level, for us to see one another. After forty minutes the intensity of fire began to relax and we were able to set course for base; of the Luftwaffe there had been no sign.

It was not then, but during the same period, that we spent our first night in France. For me it was the first since late April 1940, when I had twice passed through Paris. Recalling those vivid spring days, I remembered how disturbed I had been at the spectacle of two urchins running races in the streets; one of them, who had tripped and fallen, instead of finishing the course as loser, bloody but unbowed, had wept and brought out a torrent of recrimination and excuses. If he is representative of his time, I had thought, these people will fare badly against those tough, sunburned, purposeful Germans. Within two months the government of France had been behaving like that obscure urchin, while in England Deacon, the Battle of Britain before him, was writing in his diary: 'Nothing much doing, only the French pack up. We shall manage: our way is paved. "The people of Israel".' Strange prophetic words, yet hardly a man in the country but had been prepared then to back that belief with his life. And the mountains had been moved by faith, for here, four years later, we were in France again.

In England the weather had made flying impossible, but over Normandy it was cloudless. To a height of several thousand feet the dust, which for days had been rising from the bridgehead at the passage of every aircraft and vehicle, hung motionless in the air, perceptible only in the enriched colours, almost like those of the desert, which the setting sun evoked.

We dispersed our aircraft and, taking our Mae Wests with us for pillows, shuffled through the loose sandy soil towards the marquees where we were to eat and sleep. Bombing was still a usual nightly occurrence, and the majority of the men slept in dug-outs of various kinds which they had improvised for themselves; in the dusk in ditches or under hedges we could hear mysterious voices, and occasionally see the light of a match or cigarette, as they talked among themselves and smoked before turning-in.

As we walked back after supper from the mess-tent to the marquee in which we were to sleep, cold pools of night air were already forming in the lingering warmth of the atmosphere, while the armfuls of hay which we gathered up for palliasses were damp with dew.

Reluctant to go to sleep when it yet seemed early, we visited the Army Liaison Officer, a Canadian, in his caravan, examined his maps and heard from him some details of the bitter fighting then in progress round Caen. The town, which we had only narrowly failed to over-run on the first day of the invasion, had since then become the principal bulwark of the German positions in Normandy. The Canadian told us of an armoured wedge driven into the enemy lines south-west of Carpiquet; the battle, he said, was one of limited objectives, and it was not intended to attempt a break-through. Yet the grumbling of the guns to the south was continuous.

Later, when I was lying on the floor of the marquee, wrapped in the three blankets supplied to us, with my Mae West for pillow, I listened to their subdued, ceaseless thunder. Sleeping, I dreamt that I was one of a number of men who were trying to creep up to the place where a large, cool-headed German soldier was defending himself. The attempt was regulated like a children's game: we were only allowed to move when he was not watching us, and only if he looked up and saw any of us move was he entitled to shoot. We formed a semi-circle round him, advancing cautiously at intervals. Occasionally he raised his rifle methodically to his shoulder and, with deliberation, shot one of us. I knew none of my companions, but they were engaged on the same enterprise as I – an endeavour to reach this unflurried German – and I was horrified at the manner in which, one after another, they fell, squirmed in agony on the ground, and then lay still. The rest of us advanced again; the distance grew shorter; others fell. It began to appear doubtful whether any would be left alive to win the game. We were close enough now to see the German clearly; he was still deliberate and unflurried in his movements. Again we advanced. With horror I watched his cold eyes move round until they had met mine. We looked at each other for a long moment, and in an agony of apprehension I waited to see if his rifle would go up to his shoulder. It did not, and he turned away.

When I awoke the false dawn was beginning to show outside the tent. In the distance the guns were still rumbling sullenly, without intermission. I felt stiff and chilled, yet happy to find that my dream was only a dream. At the time I gladly averted my thoughts from its unpleasant recollection, and it was only long afterwards that I realised how much that was symbolic had occurred in it.

*

June had been as cloudy and wet as a summer month well could be, and the first half of July was hardly better. There was much bombing to be done: tactical bombing of the enemy positions round the bridge-head, strategic bombing of his lines of communication, defensive bombing of the pilotless-aircraft launching sites: and there was never any lack of work for us when weather permitted operations to take place.

On 20th July, during a brief spell of perfect weather, after escorting American medium-bombers to a marshalling-yard in Sauterne, east of Beauvais, in the morning, we took off again in the afternoon to act as cover in the Dieppe area for a small force of Lancasters which were to bomb launching-sites. We flew south-east at a comfortable 170-180 mph, climbing at the rate of 1,000 feet a minute; at ground level the cockpit was uncomfortably hot, so it was a relief to reach the colder layers of the upper atmosphere. Visibility was very good, and by the time we were half-way across the Channel, at 10,000 feet, we could see the whole sweep of the French coast, from the Somme estuary in the east to Cap d'Antifer in the west, as an unbroken line. It was difficult to believe that this ledge, which looked no deeper in section than the edge of a crazy-pavement, was constituted of dominant, towering cliffs.

At 18,000 feet changing course and direction several times to deceive predicted flak, we bore southward and crossed the coast between St Valéry and Dieppe; flying east and west, at that height, in a loose line-abreast formation, we began to patrol and waited for the bombers. As we flew back towards Dieppe from the east, we spotted them, at a lower height, crossing the coast west of the town. There were twenty-four of them in two formations; the first box turned port and began to run up to the target. As I watched, I saw about ten bursts of heavy flak appear round them. There was nothing unusual in these compact black puffs of smoke; as the moments went by, they gradually dispersed, losing their colour and menace; these I had seen before a hundred times.

What, however, immediately caught my eye was a momentary flash on the body of one of the Lancasters. I was uncertain at first whether a hit had been scored, or whether it was the effect of the sun – common enough on a bright day – glinting on perspex. Certainly the glow had seemed redder, and more lasting than the usual perspex-flash. We were on opposite courses, and soon I could see that a pinpoint of light was still showing; this could only mean that the aircraft had been hit and was on fire.

I knew how swiftly and terribly fire did its work in the air, and I waited to see if the pilot would succeed in extinguishing it. But the pinpoint not only remained but grew in size; by this time we were near enough to see that it was either a petrol-tank or an engine in the port wing which was burning. Its hold appeared so firm that I felt the aircraft was already doomed and, knowing how a burning engine, acting like a blow-lamp, can melt a main-spar in a matter of seconds, I expected every instant to see the crew abandon the machine. If they did not do so soon, it might be too late, for the port wing would clearly not last long, and few men succeed in forcing their way out of a crippled aircraft, which is falling out-of-control. Something white shot back in the slip-stream, and I thought it must be the first parachute, but it proved only to be a ring of white smoke.

Normally in the air, one cannot concentrate for long on any spectacle however interesting it may be in itself outside the routine of immediate duty; to do so runs counter to all training and instinct. On this occasion, however, by exception, I found myself absorbed in this terrible drama, unable to take my eyes from it. It was perhaps forty seconds after we had first seen the aircraft hit that it passed beneath us, flying unsteadily, as if no longer under human control, with the fire feeding hungrily on the port wing; it was close enough for us to discern every detail.

Although I had been expecting the end at every moment, I was surprised when it actually came. The Lancaster had hardly emerged in view behind the trailing-edge of my main plane before its tail-unit began to break up; a flaming fragment, probably the elevator, fluttered away from the main structure. The effect was instantaneous: the nose fell and the aircraft began to go down in a series of great swooping dives.

The flames, fanned by this forced draught, doubled and re-doubled their hold upon the machine, until the whole centre-section, and both wings as far as the outboard engines, were engulfed in fire.

If the crew had not escaped by this time they would never do so, I thought: the aircraft was wholly out of control, the fuselage a mass of flames, the forces of acceleration, in those swoops and partial recoveries, too strong for any man to fight against. I searched the sky beneath me to see if any parachutes had opened; there were none. What was it, I wondered, that had cost these men their lives: devotion? over-confidence? refusal to leave wounded comrades? a moment's hesitation? No one would ever know. How unpredictable fate was: sometimes thousands of rounds were fired at formations of hundreds of aircraft and not one was lost; to-day ten rounds had been fired at a dozen machines and, within a minute, the aircraft's fate was sealed.

Thousands of feet below the Lancaster, only visible now as a ball of fire, continued to fall. Impersonal emotion, in my experience, is not commonly felt in the air, yet I found myself deeply awed at the time, and haunted afterwards, by the spectacle of that tragic holocaust. To go down, irrevocably trapped in that inferno: it was a terrible end, past contemplation yet not a mean or undignified one. All France, between the lower Seine and Somme, must have witnessed it.

VI

The morning of 18th July on which I awoke to find the early sunshine streaming into my tent, was typical of what summer, at its best, can give: the air in our meadow felt fresh and sweet, the sky overhead was almost cloudless, and the whole Sussex countryside, downland and flat coastal strip, was steeped in a kindly, mellow light.

Overhead, however, a long stream of black Lancasters and Halifaxes, foreign to that halcyon morning, were already flying southward. Feeling surprised that we had not been called to take part in what was clearly a major operation, I dressed and drove down to the briefing-room, to learn there that the aircraft which we had seen passing overhead were part of the first wave of what was at that time to be the heaviest blow ever struck from the air in support of an army. More than a thousand British heavy-bombers, supported by six hundred American Liberators, were to lay south-east of Caen a carpet of bombs over which three armoured divisions were to pass in a thrust designed to break the enemy's hold on that city.

The main weight of bombs was to be delivered by Bomber Command on the defended villages and strong-points which lined, on east and west, the corridor of the proposed advance; these areas were to be crushed under a massive attack in which heavy demolition-bombs would be used. The passage between these two areas was to be treated with a different technique; craters would impede our tanks in their subsequent advance, so the Liberators were to lay along it a carpet of lighter metal. The operation, we all saw at a glance, was not only the largest but the most ambitious one yet attempted with the strategic bomber-forces; it would require perfect timing and a very high order of aiming if it was to be successful. Any serious blunder might jeopardize part or all of the three armoured divisions which, drawn up behind the bomb-line, were waiting for their zero-hour. Our part in the operation, we discovered, was to provide fighter-cover for part of the force of Liberators; there was just time for a hurried breakfast before it was time to take-off.

We all felt tremendous excitement and elation at the thought of this gigantic operation. It was six weeks since D-day and, after the initial successes, the battle seemed to be in danger of solidifying as those of the last war had done. We knew, of course, that there must be a long period of accumulation before decisive battles could be fought but, since the process did not go forward under our eyes, it was perhaps natural that we should have been depressed by the apparent stagnation of the fighting. At this period the British front was still held up in the east by Caen, the lynch-pin of the whole German position in Normandy, while in the west the Americans, though they had stormed Cherbourg, were yet bottled up in the Cotentin Peninsula. The limited thrusts which had been attempted up to that time had met resistance, always described as fierce, and had made little headway. But that period was ended now. The weather probably had some effect in raising our spirits: after six weeks in which it had seldom been other than a hostile witness to Allied progress, it seemed as if a change had at last taken place. I was too excited to eat much and felt glad that we were to take off almost immediately.

When we reached Caen, the ground east of the town was hardly visible through the great pall of brown dust which hung sombrely over it. We passed over the town and began to patrol as a Wing. We three squadrons were flying in line-abreast between 18,000 and 20,000 feet on an east-to-west line beyond it. Wave after wave of Liberators was coming in to bomb from the north; after bombing they all wheeled starboard in loose turns and disappeared northward beyond Bayeux. There were twelve aircraft in each wave, and they seemed to come on, apparently interminably, at precisely regulated intervals.

Each formation was greeted by a fresh outburst from the German gunners; the sun was so bright that there was nothing spectacular in the flak, as there had been during the dusk raid eleven days earlier, but it looked vicious and unpleasantly thick. We admired the

unflurried, symmetrical formation which the Americans maintained, both on the run-up and the withdrawal; to the Germans
below, wearing-out their gun-barrels that morning, the spectacle
must have been daunting in the extreme.

At one moment I spotted aircraft directly below us and led the
squadron down to investigate; they proved, however, to be
Thunderbolts, engaged on ground-attack in the enemy's rear areas.
The Luftwaffe failed to send even one formation to challenge the
operation. After forty minutes on patrol, we watched the last wave of
Liberators bomb and turn north for home; the fire from the ground
died down again; over Caen, and the terrain east of it, the gigantic
cloud of dust and smoke had risen several thousand feet and now
hung below us in the sunshine motionless. I set course north-west to
follow the bombers and, as I did so, happened to catch a fleeting
glimpse of the muzzle-flashes of a battery firing on the ground; I
did not believe that they would be aiming at us after blazing away
for two hours at more profitable targets, but took the precaution of
losing 500 ft in height. The half-dozen bursts, when they appeared,
several seconds later, were slightly above and slightly behind us.

As we flew home, I reflected that most Englishmen were then
finishing their breakfasts, yet already that day 7,500 tons of bombs
had fallen on the German lines and positions in an area not six
miles square. In April 1942, at the peak of the battle of Malta, the
Luftwaffe had required the whole month to deliver 6,700 tons of
bombs on the island. And Dunkirk: What would the effect of such
an attack as this have been on the beaches? The thought did not
suffer contemplation. What a weapon this air-power was: a
sledge-hammer constantly poised over the Wehrmacht's head! And
what a boomerang it had proved to the Germans!

This was the threat with which they had hypnotised one half of
Europe, the instrument with which they had bludgeoned the other
half into submission. Theirs, they had said, was the master-race
which had produced von Richthofen, and later Mölders and
Galland; they were invincible in the air, and any nation which
opposed them was courting apocalyptic disaster. Not only were their
pilots on pedestals of achievement beyond the capacities of lesser
breeds, but the technical development of their aircraft was, by a
decade, ahead of the world's. And behind pilots and aircraft, they

had always been at pains to proclaim, stood an industry so massive and modern that there were practically no limits to what it could achieve. Germany had forged a new weapon which had revolutionized warfare and with it, at a blow, she could strike down any nation in Europe. The Germans were indisputable masters of this new element; air-power was the sword of German destiny.

Surely here was the swiftest and most just retribution in history.

The first reports which we heard of the new offensive were startling: a clean break-through had been achieved, it was stated, and our reconnaissance troops were already on the outskirts of Falaise. Having witnessed the gigantic preparations made for it, such an advance seemed feasible, indeed probable, and the rumours were given more belief than they deserved. When the true facts were learnt later, we were, in consequence, more disappointed than we need have been. The German defences in this sector were, in fact, disposed in much greater depth than was known; the bombing therefore, while it almost completely neutralised the forward positions, left those in the rear areas untouched. The tanks, when their turn to advance came, made very rapid progress for six miles and then ran into accurate and unyielding defences beyond the limits of the bomb-pattern. Believing at the time that this was the thrust which was designed to break the ring round the bridge-head, it was natural that we should feel disappointment at seeing it held; its object, in fact, was not to break into France, but to gain the high ground south of Caen so that the enemy should be compelled to abandon the city. It was not wholly successful in this aim, but it did gain enough ground to make easier the task of the Canadians when they stormed the *faubourg* of Vancelles some days later.

The bombing was accurate and, as far as it went, devastating; little effective resistance was offered by the enemy, with one exception, in any of the focal-points of the attack, and the terrain which had been bombed was speedily and cheaply over-run. Casualties only became heavy when the advance progressed beyond the bounds of the bombardment. About five thousand prisoners were taken; of these seventy per cent could not be interrogated until two days later because they were quite deaf.

Soon after this operation the weather broke again; on the third day of rain and low-clouds the squadron was released from duty in the afternoon and the Dukes took me to have supper with the Parsons, the English family who had adopted them.

The Dukes were Canadian twins, known without distinction – for few could distinguish one from the other – by a name which was neither theirs nor that of the parents who had christened them, Bruce and Douglas. The origin of the nickname was not known; nor was it certain who was the elder, but Bruce was known as Duke I and Douglas as Duke II. Their father and mother were of Ulster and Rhineland descent respectively, and they had grown up on a farm in Alberta. They were the same height to an eighth of an inch, the same weight to a couple of pounds, always dressed alike and, though different in characters, were as similar physically as two peas. Everything they did they did together, and everything they had they shared; even their bank-balance was common to both. As pilots they had the right mixture of determination, discretion and dash to be successful and formidable; between them, they organized and had 'A' Flight.

On the ground, while not overburdened with academic learning, indeed they often made heavy weather in the pronunciation of unfamiliar words, they both had vigorous enquiring minds and little patience with tradition-bound methods or ways of thought. They had remained together practically throughout their careers in the service, and liked to say that if they had not both joined up, but only one, they could have worked alternate weeks. They were typical of their trade in never taking exercise, but unusual in that they neither smoked nor drank; photography was their main pre-occupation and delight. They represented the New World at its best.

And each, with an impartiality and detachment which was sometimes puzzling, called the other 'Duke'.

The Parsons, who entertained us, were a family, like hundreds of thousands of others in England, living on moderate means, in a house of moderate size, cultivating a garden of moderate extent. They did not live in a suburb, but in a village, yet their way of life was one which, before the war, was habitually decried as suburban. In those days it was customary, I do not know why, to derogate the suburbs and all who lived in them; no charge was too serious to be levelled at the inhabitants. They were said to be narrow in their interests, uncultivated, lacking in taste or imagination, without creative power, unadventurous, devoid of the daring which wears picturesque clothes, or falls into magnificent vices, yet in small things meanly emulative, and withal class-conscious, snobbish, morally cowardly, physically undistinguished, in short as dull as their streets, faintly ridiculous like the names of their houses.

Of such as these were said to be were the Parsons. Where repute would have them to be class-ridden and snobbish, the Dukes had found them simple and, to them, the most hospitable people in England. They had, in effect, been adopted as members of the family. A bed was always ready for them, or a meal, or a bath, or anything else they asked for; they were at liberty to come and go as they pleased, to store their surplus luggage, to eat the fruit of the garden, and even to turn the house upside down in their frenzies of developing, printing and enlarging photographs. Mrs Parsons went so far as to write to their mother, whom she had of course never met, the letters which they were too lazy to write themselves.

And instead of narrow minds and stunted imaginations, the Dukes found, beyond mere hospitality, a breadth of sympathy and interest which not only sought to see life as they did, but was able to catch their humour, suit itself to their moods and, unassumingly, to fill their needs, spiritual as well as material. And all this was done with such simplicity, kindliness, such sterling integrity, with such complete lack of affectation or ulterior motive, that it was difficult not to feel warmed to see it.

And were they, these people and the class they represented, really unadventurous and physically mediocre? I thought, as I had often thought, of the environments from which the pilots I had known came. What was it a pilot needed? Good hands, a good eye, a little education, guts, and a sense of adventure; nothing more. Any good games player, in fact, had in him the makings of a pilot, and Whitechapel started even with Mayfair. If ten years ago, I had been asked to guess which sections of the community would supply the greater numbers of our aircrews, I would have said that all should contribute equally, but that the physical advantages of the aristocrat and the outdoor worker might give them certain advantages. The timber, it would have been fair to suppose, which went to make jockeys, undergraduates, sailors, gentleman farmers, gamekeepers or poachers, transport-drivers or racing-motorists, amateur

The author off-duty.

steeplechasers or stable boys, would prove most suitable for building pilots: clerks, salesmen, office-workers, draughtsmen, on the other hand, would seem to be the worst fitted for the task.

Yet it was from this unexpected quarter that the majority of pilots had in fact come. It had been a constant cause of surprise to me, when looking through their papers, to find how many came from environments which could not, superficially, have seemed less suited to preparing them for their new lives. Where one expected to find backgrounds in which the seeds of daring, desperation, adventure, gambling, recklessness and devil-may-care had been planted, one discovered instead conventional respectability accompanied very often by marriage or engagement, and a routine, usually clerical, job.

There was no denying the fact that the majority of English pilots came from staid, middle-class homes. At one end of the scale there were few who, had they been in the Army, would have been in other than Line Regiments; at the other, the numbers springing from working-class families was both absolutely small and proportionately negligible. Nor would this near-monopoly of the middle-classes be explained in terms of snobbery or social discrimination of any sort in squadrons, where Englishmen rubbed shoulders with men of all the Dominions and any three of half-a-dozen Allies, such a factor was unknown.

These pilots were not beyond the common-stature, but in physique and spirits they probably constituted as rich a cream as their generation had to give. Without ostentation, complaint or heroics, or any form of compulsion other than that which they themselves supplied, without even requiring to be disciplined, they had voluntarily taken on themselves a task which, throughout the war, had exacted and was still exacting the heaviest toll of casualties suffered in any service or any campaign. And the majority of them had grown up in just such prosaic, conventional homes as these.

*

We had a supper of cold meats and salad which, when it was finished, we all helped to clear away. While our hostess was busy with the washing up, Mr Parsons showed me round the garden; I did not mention that Mrs Parsons had already done this, for I could see that, while there was attachment to the house, it was the garden, with its fruit-trees, little lawn, and ornamental pool, which was the main source of the family's pride and interest. It was left to the Dukes to show me the house, but the tour of the garden must be made with both Mr and Mrs Parsons.

Again my heart warmed to them: if it was anywhere, here was modern England. It was not, on the face of it, the same England as that of the Elizabethans, or of Cromwell, or of Clive, or of Wellington, or of Gordon. And yet, in the Battle of Britain, it had won complete victory against a more formidable, implacable and ruthless enemy than any of them had ever faced. It was an England which was not cultured or clever, yet it had diligence and a sense of balance; it was an England which was not brilliant or erudite, yet it possessed sanity and an ability to see both sides of a question. It was an England in which, its critics said, artistic and creative powers were dead, yet it produced a whole race of artistic and creative gardeners. It was an England which, while it had perhaps lost the single-minded fervour of Drake or Nelson, had also outgrown the moral immaturity that had permitted one to leave the Armada to its own devices for a space while he went in search of booty, and the other to dedicate his life not only to duty but to an ephemeral shadow called glory.

Above all these things, it was an England which had inherited a sense of justice and decency, of toleration, and self-control, of humour and sanity; and these, in a world of lies, brutality, exaggeration, oppression, deceit, and mindless fanaticism, seemed to me to be worth all the virtues of Bloomsbury, Paris and Munich put together.

It was at this time that we first heard that Keith Lofts, who had commanded the squadron before me, had returned safely to England. He had been shot down by flak in the Bayeux area and had crash-landed near the coast; wearing the white sweater in which he always flew, he had been seen to step out of the wreckage, rather shakily apparently, and make for cover. We knew that coastal belt to be thick with Germans, and never believed, conspicuous as he was, and dazed, that he would succeed in making his escape.

On 24th July he visited us. I knew him well, and found him none the worse for his experience; in fact he looked remarkably fit. Only his hair, which he always wore long, had grown uncut for more than two months, and was by then almost Byronic.

Having evaded capture after his crash-landing, he had been sheltered by a number of French families and, by discarding his uniform and donning civilian clothes, he had been able to pass himself off as a Frenchman. For six weeks after the invasion, he had been living in and about Caen, always trying to make his way through the enemy lines, sometimes separated from our own only by the river, yet never quite able to worm his way past the thick German defences. He told us of the fighting he had witnessed, from the first light clashes, when British and German were both racing to take possession of Caen, to the stubborn battles which had later raged round the city when it had become the hinge of the whole enemy line; he described his life in hiding, the food he had been given, the help he had received, the patrols he had eluded, and of how from the ground he had witnessed the two great Bomber Command raids on the area.

Maudsley, the squadron doctor, who knew the value of relaxation, insisted that the event should be celebrated with a party; an early release from duty was therefore procured for the squadron, liberty transport arranged, and a private room ordered. Venus was invited to join us, and that night there sat down, to the best dinner any of us had enjoyed for months, half-a-dozen Englishmen, four Canadians, two Australians, a New Zealander, a Norwegian [Gran], an Irishman and a Pole.

While the port and an unexpected green Chartreuse were circulating, we all made speeches, but it was left to the Pole, Michael Kolubinski, in his quaint, fluent yet inaccurate, English to remark on the astonishing fact that here we were, the representatives of seven different countries, not only living amicably together, but so accustomed to doing so that we did not give the matter a second thought. He said that he, and all his countrymen, would always feel grateful to the Royal Air Force, not merely in coming to their assistance when they most needed it, and in giving them aircraft, and equipment, and all the facilities they desired, but much rather because they had been welcomed into the Service, not as poor relations who had fallen on evil times, but as equals in a community in which there were no distinctions of race or nationality or creed or birth; that he himself would remember this as long as he lived, and that all men should take notice of it as a portent of what might one day prove to be a better world. The warmth of the applause which greeted this speech was genuine enough, but the faint embarrassment which the implied praise brought with it quickly sought relief in ironic humour.

We were liable to operate at dawn next day, so the party was not unduly prolonged and, after a final round, we drove home to our tents.

In spite of the twinge of embarrassment, I felt glad that Michael had made his speech; it was not the compliment to the Service, though that was graceful enough, that had warmed me, but the perception and gratitude which lay behind it. What an incalculable factor nationalism was. Some series of events built up an atmosphere which, at the touch of a trivial spark, would break-out into the great prairie fires of nationalism, sweeping over peoples, engulfing them in spite of themselves. Reason melted, truth was overwhelmed. Men at the ends of the earth would see the loom of these gigantic beacons and, as had happened to me, feel themselves compelled to answer their call. In the name of patriotism every crime could be committed, every trust betrayed, every brutality condoned, every perversion of the truth sanctified, and withal the same patriotism had the power, as had no other human motive, sacred or profane, to inspire men in the mass to unknown heights of fortitude, endurance, heroism and sacrifice.

And yet was it true to say that love of country directly inspired these qualities? At certain critical phases perhaps it did so: no one who was in England in the summer of 1940 could deny that an electric current of patriotic fervour then ran through the country and that it lifted men above their work-a-day levels. But it was an emotion too high-pitched and impersonal to be sustained indefinitely; it was an intoxication which had carried the country through these disastrous days until, by the autumn, the danger of annihilation had been removed. The bleak prospect of 1941, however, when it had become apparent that a war not lost was not the same thing as a war half-won, removed the last of its invigorating effects, and bequeathed only the reaction. Then, and for the rest of the war, it was not this ideal that inspired men; the ideal might induce them to accept a life in which heroism, fortitude and sacrifice were continually asked of them, but in finding these qualities they would discover that they had to call, not on the mystical exaltation of spirit which they had perhaps once or twice experienced, but on their own springs of nervous energy and powers of self-control.

It was patriotism that summoned men from near and far to the battle-field; it was patriotism that aligned them in two arrays, one against the other; it was patriotism that gave zest and vigour to the first charges and engagements; it was patriotism that threw over the scene a false light of grandeur and majesty, setting it, as it were, against a backcloth on which was shown every distance-enchanted epic in history; but it was only when the battle had been irrevocably joined, and the lurid illuminations of Valhalla had been replaced by sober daylight, that the contestants began to face the realities of their situation.

Some refused to recognize that they had been deceived and, playing the piece to a finish, died with a catch-word on their lips. But the majority of men, though their belief in their cause might remain undiminished, and their determination to fight for it unshaken, found that patriotism, while it was a powerful influence at the cross-roads of their lives, was not a staff which they could take with them and on which, as their path became steeper and harder, they could lean upon more and more heavily. And so men found, in war as in peace, that they were thrown back upon the resources of their own characters: the strong were strong still, but the weak had not lost their weakness.

What an inexplicable, paradoxical force it was, this love of country. Create a squadron manned by pilots of one nationality, and what did you get? Not the harmonious, fervid company you might expect, but a unit, not always at one with itself, in which national failings seemed to develop more rapidly than national virtues. Take this combustible element, patriotism, however, confine it in a restricted space, a squadron, mix it with half-a-dozen similar elements, subject it to unusual pressure, in fact do everything in your power to invite detonation, and what was the result? Not the explosion you expected, but the distillation of a new and finer spirit. That at least was the experience of the Royal Air Force, by common agreement, within its squadrons.

A paradoxical force: when you attempted to isolate it for analysis, it vanished. And yet, in our present development, it was one of the most powerful factors in human affairs: an international brigade of idealists might number its recruits by hundreds; a national army, even if it had no just cause and no ideals, enrolled its volunteers by millions. And this patriotism, which had the power to awake in the hearts of men, as religion once did, the mystical urge to welcome hardship and sacrifice, what had it produced? Not the greatest achievements, but the greatest disasters, in history.

*

On 30th July Bomber Command staged its third major intervention in the Battle of Normandy. The long period of accumulation was over and, while the British and Canadians in the east were still holding down the greater part of the enemy's weight in armour, the Americans in the west had broken through and were advancing on Avranches, at the base of the Cotentin Peninsula. It was not difficult to sense that we were on the threshold of great events.

We were woken at dawn for early breakfast and briefing. Our task, we discovered, was to fly as close-escort to 200 Lancasters, part of a force of 700 which was to bomb a corridor through the German defenses in the Caumont area; passing along this corridor, a British Armoured Division was to drive south in the direction of Vire and thereby cover the flank of the main American advance further to the west.

The morning had been bright and exhilarating, with an almost autumnal tang in it, but as we drove to our aircraft after briefing a thick blanket of cloud rolled in from the sea, so low that it almost had the effect of fog. Venus was away and, in his absence, it rested with me to decide whether or not the weather was fit for four squadrons to take-off.

It was an uncomfortable decision to have to make. I telephoned the weather-experts and asked them what was likely to happen in the next two hours; they told me that conditions were unfit for flying at most of the south-coast aerodromes, but that the cloud would lift and disperse later in the morning. At what time? They could not tell, probably by eleven o'clock. What were actual conditions in Normandy? They did not know for certain: their last report was favourable, but it was several hours old. I went outside to see whether there had been any change; the cloud might have rolled away as suddenly as it had appeared. But conditions were the same: the sun was hidden by a curtain of damp vapour and the crisp morning had become chill and uninviting; in the north, the Downs were shrouded in cloud, while to the west the spire of Chichester Cathedral was barely visible. Overhead we could hear the engines of the first waves of Lancasters; the decision would have to be made quickly.

There were three possible courses: to allow all four squadrons to take off, to allow a reduced force to take off, to forbid any aircraft to take off. If we failed to provide escort, the bombers, which were already on their way, might suffer at the hands of enemy fighters; on the other hand, if all four squadrons took the air and climbed through cloud, any further deterioration in conditions might preclude their return. The Normandy airstrips might be enjoying good conditions or they might not: it was impossible to tell. And in England in a couple of hours the cloud might have cleared or it might not: again there was no knowing. I wondered if the cloud had really lifted a little while I had been watching it, or whether my imagination was working. In any case it was impossible to stand any longer searching for a change; the other squadrons were waiting for a decision, and we should have been in our cockpits five minutes ago. I directed that we and one of the Norwegian squadrons should take off, and that the other two squadrons were to stand-by to follow us if I decided in the air that conditions were suitable.

I jumped into my aircraft, hurriedly strapped myself in, started the engine and taxied to the runway. There was something pleasantly reassuring in going through these familiar movements: man is a creature of habit, who invariably derives comfort from the familiar and is ill-at-ease with the unknown. Now that this decision had been taken, I felt less concerned with it, as if the responsibility had thereby been transferred to another. It proved, in the event, to have been the right one. I was able to call the other squadrons to follow us, and we easily over-hauled the bombers before they had reached the target.

Over France there was 9/10th of broken cloud between 1500 and 6000 ft. We expected to see the Lancasters bomb through it, but to our surprise they began to lose height until the whole stream, like the children behind the Pied Piper of Hamelin, disappeared from sight. As close-escort we were bound to follow, and so, staying well out on the flanks to avoid interfering with their bombing-runs, we followed them down, through a funnel in the cloud, to 1500 ft. Here we witnessed, in the intimacy which the weather imposed upon us, the delivery of 1000 tons of bombs, on a narrow front, in an onslaught which lasted less than five minutes. The defences seemed to have been overwhelmed by the weight of the blow and we noticed little flak; the chief risks came from collision, not only with other aircraft, but with the sticks of bombs which were raining down on all sides.

Next day, we heard that the armoured division which had passed successfully through the gap, stood in the outskirts of Vire. And to the west, the Americans had captured Avranches, the key which was to open all France to the Allies.

Notes to Part Two

Page 151
Canadian Colonel – Lt-Colonel John McCrae. The poem is 'In Flanders Fields', 1915. He died in hospital on 28 January 1918.

Page 161
Christie – Major W. Christie, OC 332 Squadron.
Lundsten – Major L. Lundsten, OC 331 Squadron.

Page 169
The Wing Commander – Lt Colonel R.A. Berg, DFC was replaced as No. 132 Wing Leader on 16th June 1944 by M. Gran, DFC.

Page 172
Venus – M. Gran, DFC.

Page 206
Keith Lofts – Wing Commander K.T. Lofts, DFC* was killed in an accident after the war.

About the Author

HUGH ANTHONY STEPHEN JOHNSTON, CMG, OBE, DFC

Extract from the Brazen Nose, the Brasenose College, Oxford, magazine for 1968/9.

[Tim] Johnston, who died after a short illness at the early age of 54 on the 9th December 1967, was born on the 7th December 1913, the son of James Johnston, Indian Civil Servant. He came to the College, as a Domus Exhibitioner, from King's College, Canterbury in 1932. He soon proved himself to be an excellent example of the good all-rounder, such as the College prided itself on fostering. He played at half in a distinguished rugger XV, was elected in 1934 a member of the Vampires (of which he became Secretary the following year), twice earned a mention in the Ale Verses, and graduated in 1935 with a very creditable Second Class in Modern Greats.

In 1936 he entered the Overseas Civil Service, in which he was eventually to make his career. This was interrupted during the war, when he served from 1940 to 1945 in the RAFVR, with characteristic gallantry and distinction; he rose to the rank of Wing Commander, and won the DFC and Bar. After returning to the Colonial Service, he was awarded the OBE in 1954 and the CMG in 1959; and his qualities received further recognition when he was appointed Deputy Governor of the Northern Region of Nigeria in 1960. The following year he returned home to become the Director of the Overseas Resettlement Bureau, a post which he held till 1965. He then entered a new occupation as Clerk to the City Parochial Foundation, and a year later published two volumes of tales which demonstrated the width of his interest in the Africa he had served – *A Selection of Hausa Stories*, and (under the name of Hugh Sturton) *Zomo the Rabbit*.

He is survived by his widow Bernice, and their children Carolyn and Robin, to whom, as to all his many friends, every sympathy is extended in their loss. Something of the impact which he made upon those who knew him is conveyed in the following tributes, which appeared in *The Times* of the 15th and 28th December last year, after his death.

'Tim Johnston's death at a tragically early age will come as a sad shock to his many friends in England and Northern Nigeria, not least to those who served with him in the Nigerian Service.

He served with great distinction in the RAF during the war. In Nigeria his fertile mind, always seeking for new ideas, his total integrity and fearlessness and his deep and sympathetic knowledge of the history and traditions of the Hausa Emirates made him an outstanding figure; to those who worked in close contact with him his great qualities of mind and character were a constant source of strength.

There are many retired Overseas Civil Service officers in England now who owe their present employment to his selfless work as Director of the Overseas Services Resettlement Bureau, to which post he was appointed after retiring from Nigeria.'*

D.H. LL.M.

'Tim Johnston had some uncommon qualities, highly developed, which would have won him wide renown if his life had been longer and if he had worked in settings where a stronger limelight falls. For myself I knew him only as the Director of the Overseas Services Resettlement Bureau, but I can testify, from weekly contacts, to his unfaltering grasp and control of his excellent instrument which he himself had largely fashioned and developed. He was tireless and insistent in his pursuit of opportunities for service at home for those who, like him, had lost these opportunities overseas. He was brave and tenacious. There was a dogged determination about him, in his stance, in his gait, in his whole demeanour and in the unfaltering gaze of those very blue eyes, twinkling with charm and humour from beneath his heavy eyebrows, but never to be deflected from the object of their gaze. He was, above most men, selflessly and entirely devoted to the "stern daughter of the voice of God".'*

G.M.

Index

Index

Airfields
  Bazenville, 174
  Bognor Regis, 149
  Coltishall, 13
  Duerne, 149
  Eglington, 14
  Ibsley, 149
  Kirton-in-Lindsey, 14
  Lille-Nord, 149
  Lympne, 189
  Neufcampville, 149
  Tangmere, 149
Alexandria, 14
Anvil Point, 164
Argus, HMS, 89
Atlantic Wall, 157, 162
Avranches, 209, 211

Baker, 31
Barflour, 155
Barnes, 26
Barton, Wng Co R.A., OBE DFC
  (Bar) (Bart), 21, 22, 90, 96, 102,
  108, 124, 126, 127, 143
Bastion, 75, 79
Battle of Britain, 154, 192, 205
Bayeux, 198, 206
Beachy Head, 152, 160, 166, 167,
  177, 178, 179, 180
Beauvais, 169, 194
Berg, Lt Col R.A., DFC, 150
Bisley, John H.E., DFC (Australia),
  57, 60, 64, 66, 68, 76, 77, 124,
  144

Bizerta, 25
Booker, 100
Booth, Douglas E., DFC, 100, 127,
  128
Boulton, 27
Brejcha (Polish pilot), 137
Brennan, Virgil P., DFC DFM
  (Bren), 122, 145
Brest, 152
Brighton, 167, 178
Brittany, 152
Brooker, 62
Brown, 166, 167, 173
Buchanan, G.A.F. (Buck), 86, 144
Busuttil, Carrie, 77

Caen, 191, 192, 197, 198, 199, 200,
  206
Calafrana, 33, 60, 61
Calvados, 165
Canada, 57, 60, 62
Cap d'Antifer, 152, 194
Cape Bon, 28
Carpiquet, 193
Castile, Valetta, 72
Caumont, 210
Charlie, (batman), 50
Cherbourg, 152, 164. 165, 198
Christie, Major W., 149, 161, 162,
  163
Cisk Brewery, 76
Connell, Bud, 46, 49
Contentin Peninsula, 152, 165, 198,
  209

Cospicua, 33
Crete, 56
Crist, Flt Sgt E.A. (Chris), 57, 60, 90, 96, 99, 106, 107, 108, 122, 124

Daddo-Langlois, Raoul, DFC, 122, 145
D-Day, 150
Deacon, 192
Delville Wood, 158
Denis, 31, 32
Dieppe, 169, 177, 178, 194
Douglas-Hamilton, Sqn Ldr Lord David (Douglas), 127, 136, 145
Douthen, 188
Duke I (Bruce), 201, 202, 205
Duke II (Douglas), 201, 202, 205
Dunkirk, 199
Dusty, 66, 106, 107

Eagle, HMS, 24, 25, 26, 27, 50, 89
Eagle Squadrons, The, 13
Eastbourne, 167
Emery, Reg, 177, 178, 179, 181
Etna, Mt, 70
Evreux, 169

Falaise, 200
Filfla, 99, 100, 106, 110
Floriana, 33, 73

Galite Island, 28
Galland, General Adolf, 139
Gilbraltar, 14, 22, 23, 33, 52
Goldsmith, Sqn Ldr A.P., DFC DFM (Goldie), 62, 74, 77, 78, 99, 108, 135, 144
Gondar, 40, 61, 66
Gozo, 30, 49, 56, 66, 124
Gracie, Sqn Ldr E.F., DFC, 14, 143
Gran, Maj M., DFC (Venus), 150, 172, 177, 189, 190, 207, 210
Grand Harbour, 33, 40, 46, 55, 66, 67, 68, 70, 73, 92, 106, 107, 111, 122, 123, 124, 134, 136

Grant, Wng Co S.B., DFC (Bar), 44, 143
Graves, Flt Lt M.A., DFC (Mike), 36, 38, 39, 40, 44, 46, 50, 70, 71, 72, 77, 103, 107, 135

Halfar, 33, 40, 50, 75, 90, 101, 105, 108, 127
Ham Run, 73
Hasting, 114
Haugland, V., 13
Heidelberg, 115, 116
Heppell, Wng Co P.W.E., DFC (Bar) (Nippy), 73, 76, 144
Hermione, HMS, 26
Hesselyn, Ray Brown, MBE DFM (Bar), 135, 145
Hughes, Shorty, 24, 106, 107, 108, 122

Illustrious, HMS, 31

Jemmet, Frank, 62, 102, 103
Jimmie, (batman), 50

Kelly, 74, 84
Killeen, 38, 97
Kolubinski, Michael, 207
Kurt (German pilot), 68, 69, 76, 86, 138, 139

Le Havre, 152
Le Tréport, 152, 178, 180, 181
Lille, 155
Lodge, John, 96
Lofts, Wng Co Keith, T., DFC (Bar), 206
Lonnan, George, 175
Lowestoft, 44
Lundsten, Major L., 149, 161, 162, 163
Luqa, 30, 32, 33, 36, 42, 44, 46, 48, 49, 50, 57, 60, 84, 86, 89, 93, 96, 99, 101, 105, 108, 112, 122, 123, 126, 139, 141

MacLeod, Donald W. (Mac), 21, 22, 38, 39, 44, 45, 50, 57, 60, 61, 62, 65, 66, 75, 76, 79, 84, 85, 143
McNair, Grp Capt R.W., DSO DFC (Buck), 49, 138, 143
MacQueen, Flt Lt N.C., DFC (MacQ), 68, 76, 84, 86, 99, 126, 127, 139, 144
Malaya, HMS, 26
Manuel, (batman), 50
Maudsley, Dr, 206
M'dina, 36, 85
Mitchell, Colonel, 132, 133, 139
Mölders, 138, 139, 199
Musta Cathedral, 48, 74, 85

Nash, PO Peter A., DFC, 50, 55, 97, 144
Nashar, 75
Neuhof, Staffel-Kapitän, 86
Newhaven, 167, 168
Norman, 31, 36, 50, 76
Normandy, 149, 152, 159, 190, 192, 193, 198, 209, 210

Old Bailey, 65, 102, 105, 124
Omaha beach, 155
Opera House, Valetta, 72
Orne river, 191

Palace Square, Valetta, 71
Palmer, Sister, 139
Pantellaria, 25, 26, 28, 30, 52
Parsons family, 201, 202, 204, 205
Peck, James E. (Jimmie), 21, 22, 38, 39, 45, 50, 52, 57, 58, 60, 61, 64, 65, 66, 76, 90, 96, 99, 108, 110, 126, 127, 143
Penelope, HMS, 70
Pete, 44, 69, 80, 135
Picardy, 152
Plagis, Wng Co John A., DSO DFC (Bar) (Johnny), 50, 55, 75, 84, 86, 135, 136, 144
Pointe de la Percée, 157

Policino, Anne, 84
Prague, 115
Public Library, Valetta, 72, 80
Putnam, Hiram A. (Tex), 62, 66, 68, 90, 96, 144

Queen Victoria, HMS, 21

Rabat, 65, 92
Richthofen, Baron von, 199
Ricky, 90, 96, 99
Rommel, F.M. Erwin, 55, 56, 140, 141, 157, 158
Romney Marsh, 189

St Catherine's Point, 156, 160
St Malo, 152
St Martin de Vanneville, 157, 158
St Paul's Bay, 91, 126
St Pol, 188
St Valéry, 194
Sandy Bay, 24
Satchell, Wng Co W.A.J., DSO, 124, 143
Sauterne, 194
Schade, Flt Sgt P.A., DFM (Malaya), 62, 90, 105, 135, 144
Scheldt, 152
Seghers, Sqn Ld E.G.A., DFC, 149
Seine Bay, 152, 155, 191, 196
Senglea, 33
Sergeant, Bob, 84, 99
Sicily, 14, 32, 47, 54, 56, 68, 71, 85, 102, 108, 124, 134, 135, 137
Sliema, 124
Sliema Creek, 33
Somme, 152, 181, 189, 196
Squadrons
  66: 149, 150
  121: 38
  126: 15, 35, 50, 140
  133: 13, 14, 62
  165: 149
  249: 32, 33, 34, 38, 46, 50, 55, 74, 96, 122, 140

257: 13, 31
331: 149
332: 149
601: 89, 122
603: 89, 127, 135
611: 149
Strada Reale, Valetta, 72
Suez Canal, 14, 56
Susa, 28

Takali, 26, 30, 31, 32, 33, 36, 48, 50, 68, 74, 75, 90, 91, 96, 97, 101, 105, 108, 113, 124, 134
Tedder, Air Marshal, 79
Tulley, Reade, DFC (Florida), 100, 127, 135, 144
Tuck, Sqn Ldr 'Bob' Stanford, DSO DFC, 13
Turner, Wng Co, 54

Uher, Polish pilot, 137
Utah beach, 155

Valetta, 26, 33, 36, 44, 65, 70, 71, 73, 76, 77, 80, 81, 102, 103, 107, 123
Vancelles, 200
Verdala Castle, 102
Vernon, 169
Vire, river, 155, 210, 211
Vittoriosa, 33

Wasp, USS, 89
Waterhouse, 170
West, Geoff, 75, 102, 103
West, Flt Lt Ronald, DFC (Ron), 73, 144
Wight, Isle of, 157, 160, 164
Woodhall, Grp Capt A.B., OBE (Woodie), 38, 39, 44, 46, 48, 49, 50, 57, 106, 110, 113, 127, 143

Zeeland, 152